# WORLD DOMINATION
THE SUB POP RECORDS STORY

D0743680

# WORLD DOMINATION

## THE SUB POP RECORDS STORY

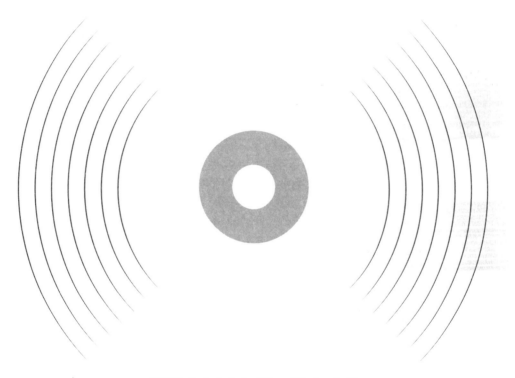

# GILLIAN G. GAAR

Cover Design by Randall Leddy

Photo credits: Black and white photos on pages P1 and P6–P11 of photo insert
by Charles Peterson. Used by permission of photographer. Color photo on
page P16 of photo insert courtesy of Bruce Pavitt. All others photos and images
courtesy of Sub Pop Records.

Library of Congress Cataloging-in-Publication Data available upon request.

ISBN: 9781947026186

Published by BMG
www.bmg.com

To Tom Kipp
record collector extraordinaire

# CONTENTS

# PROLOGUE
## The Twentieth Anniversary

*But really, did anyone expect a little label like Sub Pop to see its 20th birthday? ... Seriously, who'd've thought it? Other than the humble founders of Sub Pop, that is?*

—Press release for Sub Pop's twentieth anniversary, April 2, 2008

### July 10, 2008, Seattle, Washington

The Space Needle, the most eye-catching structure built for the 1962 World's Fair, has become the kind of architectural icon that immediately identifies its city. Like Big Ben or the Eiffel Tower, as soon as you see it, you know the location. And for the Space Needle, that location is Seattle.

Today, the Space Needle attracts over a million visitors a year, who ride up elevators that travel at the speed of ten miles an hour to visit either the observation deck or the rotating restaurant. Unsurprisingly, the Space Needle has also been the focal point for numerous local celebrations over the years: lights strung from the antenna on top to form a Christmas tree during the holidays, the logo of the University of Washington Huskies football team painted on the Needle's roof when the team won the Rose Bowl in 1992, the Seattle Seahawks' "12th Man" flag flying from the antenna whenever the football team makes it to the Super Bowl, and fireworks set off from the structure's top on New Year's Eve.

But it was still something of a jolt to see a giant flag with the logo of Sub Pop Records rippling in the breeze atop the Needle in the summer of 2008, in celebration of the company's twentieth anniversary. (The observation deck's roof was even painted to look like a record label, with the words, "Thank You, Seattle. Love, Sub Pop.") After all, Sub Pop wasn't a major holiday or a huge business franchise; it was a scrappy record company. One that constantly struggled to avoid bankruptcy during its early years. One that defiantly thumbed its nose at the prevailing "greed is good" consumerist culture of the 1980s by producing T-shirts sporting the single word "LOSER." One that perversely seemed to take more pride in its potential for failure than the results of its success, as seen in one of the company's slogans: "Going out of business since 1988."

Yet there they are, Sub Pop's co-founders, Bruce Pavitt and Jonathan Poneman, chatting with friends and supporters at the celebratory party held at the Needle's Skyline restaurant (a mere one hundred feet from the ground, in contrast to the main restaurant, which is at the five-hundred-foot level). It's the first day of events commemorating Sub Pop's twentieth anniversary, which began a few hours previously, with Bruce and Jon appearing at what was then called the Experience Music Project (a music/entertainment industry museum founded by Microsoft billionaire Paul Allen, renamed the Museum of Pop Culture in 2017). The two sat for a public interview with EMP curator Jacob McMurray, destined for the museum's oral history archives.

Bruce and Jon looked back at a time when touring bands used to give Seattle a miss, which added to the city's "regional isolation," in Bruce's words—but how that very isolation fueled a sense of community that led to the creation of a distinctive "Seattle sound." They also recalled the more practical concerns of trying to keep a record company afloat during that first, fraught month of April 1988.

"I was there when Jonathan struggled with the representative from the phone company," Bruce remembered, "arguing for half an hour that they really shouldn't pull the plug on our service. And that, indeed, we would be paying them sometime. And I knew that a record label without phone service would essentially be defunct. And this gentleman, with his superior negotiating skills, bought us an extra ten days."

There was also a surprise guest in the house: Seattle mayor Greg Nickels, who read aloud the city's official proclamation naming July 11–14 as "Sub Pop's Utterly Lost Weekend," further urging the city's residents to "join me in celebrating Sub Pop's questionable taste in music, generous nature, and improbable solvency."

"Who wrote that proclamation?" Jon joked afterward. "Because it was a wonderful marketing opportunity seized. I love it. A few more bands could have been mentioned."

Later, at the Skyline restaurant party, past and present Sub Pop employees and band members reconnect: musician/producer Steve Fisk, the Fastbacks' Kim Warnick, Mark Pickerel of Screaming Trees, and Carla Torgerson of the Walkabouts. Kelley Stoltz, Death Vessel, and Sera Cahoone provide musical entertainment, though attendees seem to spend most of their time waiting in the long drinks lines. There's even a special beer created for the occasion: Loser Pale Ale, by the Seattle-based Elysian Brewing Company, a sweet, hoppy brew, with its 6.5 percent alcohol content providing a nice kick. (It was later boosted to 7 percent.) In keeping with Sub Pop's special brand of humor, the beer's labels bear the slogan "Corporate Beer Still Sucks."

◎ ◎ ◎

Meanwhile, across town, there's a revival going on. Green River, who released their first Sub Pop record twenty-one years earlier, have reunited, performing a warm-up show at the Sunset Tavern, in advance of their appearance at SP20, a festival of Sub Pop acts being held over the weekend. After breaking up in 1987, the band has only reunited once before, during an encore at a Pearl Jam concert in Las Vegas on November 30, 1993.

But that performance didn't feature all the original members. This one does: vocalist Mark Arm, bassist Jeff Ament, drummer Alex Vincent, and all the guitarists who ever played in the band: Steve Turner, Stone Gossard, and Bruce Fairweather. Mark Arm doesn't pull the same stunts he used to during Green River's heyday. (At one show, he leapt from the stage to swing on a light fixture suspended from the ceiling, which began breaking apart. "Not one of my brightest moments," he notes. "I was pretty high on MDA.") But he does manage to dive into the audience, later resurfacing on the bar. The crowd moshes like it's 1989, even attempting a little stage diving, though most of those present seem to have outgrown such tomfoolery.

The SP20 Festival officially opens the next night, July 11, with a comedy show at the Moore Theatre. "Happy birthday, Mr. Sub Pop!" announces host Kristen Schaal (at the time best known for her appearances on the TV series *Flight of the Conchords*) as she kicks off the evening. "And the weather is perfect today—even if this is the suicide capital of the world." The Moore Theatre is an especially appropriate location, as it was also the site of Sub Pop's first "Lame Fest," held on June 9, 1989, and featuring a bill of Nirvana, TAD, and Mudhoney. That show drew a sellout crowd of fifteen hundred, which Bruce and Jon quickly took note of; here was the proof that they had tapped into a receptive audience.

Tonight's comedy show illustrates how the label's interests have broadened. As a company that never seemed to take itself too seriously, Sub Pop was always something of a comedy label, even before it signed an actual comedian. Now the roster boasts the likes of David Cross and Patton Oswalt (both of whom are performing this evening), and the Flight of the Conchords comedy duo Jemaine Clement and Bret McKenzie.

On Saturday, July 12, the action moves outdoors to Marymoor Park in Redmond, a Seattle suburb (and home to Microsoft's headquarters), for the first of two all-day events. SP20 is certainly not a nostalgia fest; evidently, the kids who grew up listening to Sub Pop's bands now see fit to bring their own progeny to this year's celebrations. It's a family-friendly event, with an adult in flannel next to a punk rocker in bondage pants and a hat sporting a pentangle next to a little girl romping around in a red dress with white polka dots. Old-timers have unearthed vintage T-shirts: Green River's "RIDE THE FUCKING SIX PACK," Soundgarden's "TOTAL FUCKING GODHEAD," and the ubiquitous "LOSER" tee (with a Sub Pop logo on the back).

There are booths supporting the usual indie/progressive causes: the Vera Project (one of Seattle's all-ages clubs), skateboarding for girls, and Obama '08. ("We've given out a few thousand stickers," a staffer notes proudly.) There's swag to be had as well: a compilation CD entitled *Happy Birthday to Me: Terminal Sales Vol. 3* (Seattle's Terminal Sales Building being the site of Sub Pop's original HQ). It's a sampler of the label's current acts, including the Ruby Suns, the Helio Sequence, the Glitter Twins (that would be Screaming Trees lead singer Mark Lanegan and Greg Dulli, singer/guitarist with the Afghan Whigs), and Sub Pop stalwarts Mudhoney, whose debut release for the label also came out twenty years ago.

Two stages have been set up side by side, allowing for quick changeovers and little downtime between sets. While Sub Pop's initial roster focused on the Pacific Northwest, the lineup at SP20 spotlights acts from around the country, including the Fluid, from Denver (who, like Green River, have reunited for the event), and Iron & Wine, originally from Florida.

There's a bit of international flavor, too, courtesy of the Constantines and Eric's Trip, both from Canada (the latter was the first Canadian act signed to the label), and the Vaselines, the Scottish duo whose bitter love songs were much beloved by Nirvana's Kurt Cobain. Indeed, it was Kurt's continual championing of the group that led to Sub Pop releasing *The Way of the Vaselines: A Complete History* in 1992, three years after the group broke up.

Saturday night closes with a set by Flight of the Conchords; those in search of still more entertainment can head back to Seattle to catch another SP20 gig at the Showbox, featuring Brothers of the Sonic Cloth (the new band founded by Tad Doyle, the mighty lead singer and guitarist from Sub Pop act TAD), and the Glitter Twins.

On Sunday, Marymoor Park's stages host appearances by acts both near (Seattle-based Kinski) and far (France's Les Thugs, who also reunited for SP20). LA alt-country act Beachwood Sparks, which broke up in 2002, is yet another group to have reformed specifically for SP20; they'll go on to release one more album for Sub Pop, 2012's *The Tarnished Gold*. There's been ongoing revelry in the backstage VIP area as well, with attendees quaffing Loser pale ale and dining on ribs, soft tacos, and Kobe beef burgers. There's Jack Endino, who produced virtually all of Sub Pop's first releases; Chad Channing, the drummer on Nirvana's Sub Pop album *Bleach*; Kevin Whitworth of Love Battery; Candice Pedersen, co-owner of Olympia-based K Records; Linda Derschang, whose first bar, Linda's, was co-owned by Bruce and Jon, and was something of a Sub Pop clubhouse during the 1990s. Soundgarden couldn't be persuaded to reunite for SP20 (that won't happen for another year and a half), but Kim Thayil and Matt Cameron are nevertheless in attendance.

Green River play in the afternoon, Mark Arm wearing the same "Green River Summer Camps" T-shirt he wore at the Sunset Tavern. "Oh my God!" one attendee shrieks in disbelief as the band takes the stage, amazed that he's actually going to see the group hailed as the "Band Who Invented Grunge."

Ah, "grunge." It's a term that's been used with both affection and disparagement. But if it wasn't for Sub Pop's success in marketing the alternative rock genre, there would be no festival today. Indeed, Sub Pop used the term in promoting the first Green River record the label released, *Dry as a Bone*, describing it as "ultra-loose GRUNGE that destroyed the morals of a generation."

Mark writhes around the stage, contorting his body like a pretzel, surpassing even Mudhoney's performance the previous day. Classics like "Swallow My Pride" and "Come on Down" are present and accounted for. Prior to "Leech," Arm playfully accuses the Melvins of stealing the song from a Green River demo and crediting it to themselves, "Making us the Willie Dixon of grunge," he says, referring to Led Zeppelin's drawing on Dixon's "You Need Love" for their "Whole Lotta Love" (Dixon sued and was eventually credited as co-author). "Luckily," Mark continues, "now that we're all back together, we've melded the legal power of Pearl Jam and Sub Pop, and we're going to crush those bastards!"

He also serves up a mini history lesson, introducing the band members by referring to their pre–Green River bands: "On my right, Bruce Fairweather and Jeff Ament from the Montana hardcore band Deranged Diction! On my left, Steve Turner and Stone Gossard from the proto-grunge band the Ducky Boys! And on the drums, Spluii Numa's own Alex Shumway! Oh—and I'm the evil genius behind Mr. Epp," he concludes, cracking a grin, well aware that most of the audience has no idea who any of these bands are. The set concludes with Alex diving into the crowd, while the rest of the band members toss brand spanking new "RIDE THE FUCKING SIX PACK" T-shirts into the audience's eager hands.

SP20 closes with Wolf Parade, a Montreal-based band that has just released a second album for the label, *At Mount Zoomer*, which hit the Canadian Top

20 (and reached no. 45 in the US). Is it odd to end a festival celebrating a Seattle label with a band from Montreal? The crowd doesn't seem to mind, having been swept up in the delirium of such numbers as "An Animal in Your Care," "I Am a Runner," and "Soldier's Grin." Their final song, "I'll Believe in Anything," from their debut album, *Apologies to the Queen Mary*, has an additional resonance on this night. After all, it was Bruce and Jon's unshakable belief in their label that kept Sub Pop going during those first rocky years, eventually resulting in the kind of phenomenal success they could have scarcely imagined when they were begging the phone company not to cut off their phone line.

◎ ◎ ◎

For a label known for its penchant for hyperbole, it was surprising that Sub Pop's co-founders didn't take the stage at some point during SP20 to engage in some self-congratulatory badinage, as they had at EMP. At that event, they'd also reflected on the personal and professional changes they'd gone through over the preceding twenty years.

"The long road that we've traveled here, I think, has been illuminating in that it's often been very humbling," Bruce said. "And we've gone through this very strange dynamic, up and down, being showered with attention and stepping into our ego, and then being beaten down and humbled the next day because we just bounced a check to our favorite employee. And you go through that a couple hundred times, and it kind of strengthens your character a little bit, and gives you some perspective. And it's been a good thing."

"The spirit of the twentieth anniversary is really not so much about Sub Pop as much as it is about our community—the culture at large," Jon explained in an interview with me shortly before SP20. "This culture, and the individuals who have participated in it, continue to thrive. And speaking for myself, I'm middle-aged. This has kind of defined my life. And these people are my family, and this company is, in many ways; it's my family, and it's been my life mission and work heretofore.

"So I don't want to make too much of it, but it's a celebration," he continued. "It's an opportunity not just for a family reunion, but for the youngsters amongst us to see even a fragment of what this all was and what it all can be. I think this culture is continually enriched by new people who come into it and bring their own experiences into it. And if this event can galvanize even a handful of people to move forward and do things like-minded then it's an absolute success. And it's an opportunity to party and hang out and have a good time."

There was no further extemporizing during the weekend itself. Instead, Bruce and Jon were just two more faces in the crowd throughout Saturday and Sunday, checking out the bands, clearly still just as interested in experiencing music the old-fashioned way as they were when they started their label. Asked by an audience member at EMP about the changing musical styles of the bands on Sub Pop over the years, Jon replied, "I think it's just the music that we like. And, from my perspective at least, the reason the music that you hear on the label is what it is, is simply because it's stuff that we like to listen to and that we're fans of." And so it was, perhaps, fitting that at SP20, the two men who had come together to release records by their friends, never dreaming of the cultural impact they might go on to have, decided to step back and let the music speak for itself.

# 1
## ROOTS

*We must all become energetic about the fact that there is great music in America; and, that some of the most truly avant-garde pop hysteria is coming out of traditionally boring environments … EXPLOSIVE artistic hanky-panky is everywhere.*

—Bruce Pavitt, *Subterranean Pop #2*, November 1980

On a summer's day in 1977, Bruce Pavitt had an experience that would alter the trajectory of his life. He was attending a barbeque in Park Forest, in suburban Chicago, when a friend dropped the needle on a newly released 45: "God Save the Queen" by the Sex Pistols. As Steve Jones's guitar intro roared out of the speakers and Johnny Rotten sneered his way through the song's first line, people dropped their beers and glared at the offending impromptu DJ. "And from that moment on, I knew that music really had the power to provoke and to shift consciousness immediately," Bruce later recalled. "And that was a life-changing event for me."

It was yet another step in a journey that would ultimately lead Bruce to oversee the release of music that also had "the power to provoke and to shift consciousness." As a child, he'd spent hours absorbing music on the radio and was a regular viewer of *The Ed Sullivan Show*, the most popular variety program on TV, which always featured at least one rock act per show. He sold Christmas cards door-to-door to save up enough money to buy a record player; once he'd acquired it, the first two singles he bought were "Revolution" by the Beatles and "Sugar, Sugar" by the Archies. In his teens, his girlfriend's brothers turned him on to punk rock. He soon tracked down Devo's first singles, "Mongoloid" and their twisted cover of the Rolling Stones' "(I Can't Get No) Satisfaction," marveling that music that sounded so strange could emanate from a place as conventional as Akron, Ohio. Picking up fanzines like *CLE*, which also came from the Buckeye State, gave him further avenues to explore.

Even the storied "Gray Lady," the *New York Times*, unexpectedly provided some leads. Bruce's father had a subscription to the paper, and reading the entertainment section tipped Bruce off to the existence of bands with quirky names like Television, the Ramones, and Talking Heads. "I wasn't reading about those groups in *Rolling Stone*," he noted. He spent time scrutinizing the inventory at Wax Trax Records on N. Lincoln Avenue in Chicago (his own tenure working in retail, in the record department of Korvettes' department store, was short-lived; he was fired a day after playing a record by the Ramones). On a visit to New York City, he watched as the B-52's played to a small but fervent audience of twenty at the legendary punk haunt CBGB. Discovering that the band was from Athens, a then-obscure college town in Georgia, added to Bruce's growing realization that regional music scenes could be just as vibrant and exciting as those in the designated cultural hotspots of New York, Los Angeles, or London. Maybe even more exciting.

So in 1979, when Bruce transferred from Blackburn College in Carlinville, Illinois, to The Evergreen State College, located in Washington's state capital of Olympia, he didn't view it as a move to an isolated community in a state that was then considered something of a cultural backwater. Instead, he regarded his new home as an environment bursting with opportunity and possibility.

◙ ◙ ◙

Evergreen, which opened in 1971, was a nontraditional university that allowed students to design their own fields of study; they also received "evaluations" from their teachers instead of grades. It was a system Bruce was accustomed to; in high school, he'd been put in an Active Learning Process School (ALPS) program that functioned in a similar fashion. "Students were expected to initiate independent studies, along with classes that emphasized discussions with students, rather than lectures," he explains.

Bruce learned about Evergreen from a fellow ALPS student. "My true academic interest came into focus at Evergreen," he says, "which was the study of independent alternative regional US scenes. By the time I graduated, I was a walking encyclopedia of underground punk and indie culture, which seemed like a ridiculous way to exit college."

His first step was to volunteer for the campus radio station, KAOS. College radio stations were known for playing music outside of the mainstream, but John Foster, the station's music director, went further, instituting a policy whereby 80 percent of the music KAOS broadcast had to be on an independent label. "That was pretty revolutionary at the time," Bruce later observed. The name of his own radio show illustrated its left-of-center focus: *Subterranean Pop*, the two words suggesting music that came from the underground but was nonetheless catchy. It aired in the prime spot of ten to midnight on Fridays.

"It was just the perfect thing to do," Bruce says of enrolling at Evergreen. "It was almost as if it was a divinely orchestrated event, because, for myself upon arriving, I realized that the radio station there had possibly the best collection of independent records in the country. And I didn't know this before I headed out to go to Evergreen. And so that was a tremendous blessing."

As he browsed the KAOS music library, Bruce was amazed at the wealth of music that was being released on records that most people would never realize even existed. "Bands like the Blackouts from Seattle, and the Neo Boys and the

Wipers from Portland [Oregon]—none of this music was making its way out to, for example, Wax Trax Records in Chicago, which was one of the best record stores in the country," he says. "Some of the best records out there were not being appreciated by anybody outside of their local region. I was so inspired that I felt I had to go beyond my *Subterranean Pop* radio show and share information about these records that a lot of people had never heard of."

Bruce found further inspiration in another of John Foster's ventures: *OP* magazine. *OP*, co-founded by Foster, had started out as an insert in KAOS's program guide before becoming a standalone publication in August 1979, just as Bruce was arriving at Evergreen. The magazine focused on independent artists, included a broad spectrum of genres, and was keyed to the alphabet: the first issue covered artists and groups whose names started with *A*, the second issue covered those whose names started with *B*, and so on. Its run stopped in 1984, after twenty-six issues.

Bruce did an internship at the magazine. He soon began thinking about doing his own publication (for which, in typical Evergreen fashion, he would get college credit as an "independent study" project), planning to focus on reviewing records on a city-by-city basis. His would also be a more low-budget effort. Unable to afford proper printing, he'd have to rely on photocopying— his would be a fanzine (more simply called a "zine"), not a magazine. In the days before the Internet, fanzines were how enthusiasts spread the word about their particular interests outside of the mainstream media, putting together a publication in the best DIY tradition: typing or even handwriting the copy, pasting articles and photos on blank sheets of paper, then photocopying them and stapling them together.

"The whole thing was put together with an X-Acto knife and press type and a typewriter," Bruce explains. "There was no spell check, so you'd see some misspelled words here and there; occasionally, if the typing got screwed up, I would take a pen and cross it out and continue typing! Super DIY. I couldn't afford to make halftones of the photos, so I'd just Xerox them two or three times until they were really grainy, and they'd reproduce in kind of a trippy, ghostly way."

The zine took the same name as Bruce's radio show, and the first issue of *Subterranean Pop* appeared in May 1980. Thirty-two pages long and priced at fifty cents, its first sentence announced, "*Subterranean Pop* is a fanzine dedicated to independent recordings from the Northwest and the Midwest." Its mission was clear: "All record reviews are highly prejudiced and reflect the personal tastes of the editor." The issue's "New Pop!! Manifesto" further expanded on the zine's raison d'être: "When people buy a record, they are not only plugging into the music, but into the values and lifestyles that are implied by that artist …. Only by supporting new ideas by local artists, bands, and record labels can the US expect any kind of dynamic social/cultural change in the 1980s."

The first issue featured reports on the music scenes in Seattle, Portland, San Francisco, Chicago, Detroit, Minneapolis, Athens and Atlanta (Georgia), Austin and Houston (Texas), and Vancouver, BC (Canada). There were also short, punchy record reviews: *Is This Real?* by Portland band the Wipers was hailed as "one of the best independent LPs to come out of the US this year," while Detroit's Algebra Mothers earned the withering description, "These guys show about as much emotion as a text book. Gimme the Archies."

Most reviews were accompanied by an address from which the reader could order the record. "Which was key," says Bruce. "Nobody was doing this, besides *OP*; you could actually mail order these records from different cities. And I figured the exchange of information would help inspire people." One page in the zine also listed addresses for record manufacturers and distributors, along with the helpful encouragement, "Making your own records is a lot cheaper than you think."

Once he had the entire print run of his first issue ready, Bruce took the kind of inspired risk that would characterize Sub Pop's attitude of going for broke against even the most insurmountable odds. Instead of sending potential distributors a copy of the zine and asking if each company would be interested in taking it on, he sent all five hundred copies to Systematic, a distributor based in San Francisco. Luckily, instead of throwing the unsolicited package into the trash, a sympathetic Joe Carducci, who ran Systematic (and would go on to work at SST Records as an A&R rep and producer), decided to carry *Subterranean Pop*—and managed to sell every copy. Bruce noted that it probably didn't hurt that his zine reviewed other items that Systematic distributed, "and *Sub Pop* was probably the only zine doing that."

◎ ◎ ◎

By the third issue, the zine had the shorter, punchier title of *Sub Pop*. "I thought it sounded better," Bruce explains. *Sub Pop*'s brief had quickly expanded beyond record reviews; subsequent issues carried information about record shops, clubs, radio stations, magazines/fanzines, and film. He also kept an eye on the alternative comics scene, with *Sub Pop* publishing work from *Raw* as well as early work by Lynda Barry and Charles Burns, both of whom had attended Evergreen.

Bruce had seen Lynda's "Ernie Pook's Comeek" in the student newspaper, the *Cooper Point Journal*, and wrote her a letter, asking if she'd do a cover illustration for him; she provided one for the second issue of *Subterranean Pop*, which was published in November 1980. "This is Lynda Barry, 1980, when she was at her punk-rock peak," Bruce notes proudly of the cartoonist, who would go on to create such illustrated works as *The Good Times Are Killing Me* and *What It Is*. "We were two Evergreen students collaborating on a little DIY zine." Barry's Evergreen-era work would later appear in the book *Blabber Blabber Blabber: Volume 1 of Everything*.

Charles Burns's work also appeared in the *Cooper Point Journal*, and he contributed to *OP* as well. Bruce had seen Charles's work in a publication from Oakland, California, *Another Room* (likely one of the first alternative publications designed on an Apple computer). Learning that Charles had attended Evergreen "gave me the nerve to write him and ask him to do something," Bruce says.

Burns's work first appeared on the back cover of *Sub Pop*'s fourth issue (a stark drawing of a man whose face has no skin, singing "Dedicated to the One I Love"). His illustrations also graced the covers of *Sub Pop*'s "cassette zines": issues five, seven, and nine. The cassettes marked the first time the "Sub Pop" name was attached not to reviews but to the actual release of music.

Bruce had begun working on *Sub Pop* with a younger Evergreen student, Calvin Johnson. Like Bruce, Calvin had a show on KAOS and shared his interest in exploring and promoting regional music. (Bruce had taken over Calvin's spot on KAOS when Calvin moved to Washington, DC, for a year.) "I was always really, really impressed with what Calvin was doing," says Bruce. "I've always thought that he had a very creative take on the world. I think he's a creative genius of sorts, and I've had a very ongoing respect for his vision."

The two had discovered an Australian cassette magazine called *Fast Forward* that featured interviews and commentary between songs, and they decided to put together something similar. As they saw it, it was a logical progression to move from writing about music to releasing it, and cassettes provided a cheap, readily accessible format. "Cassettes are the ultimate tool," Bruce wrote in *Sub Pop 4*, in soliciting songs for the first *Sub Pop* compilation. "Unlike records, production and manufacturing can happen—within minutes— in your own living room(!)"

*Sub Pop 5*, released in July 1981, featured twenty-one tracks, half from the Pacific Northwest, the rest from around the country: Milwaukee; Dallas; Wichita, Kansas; Saratoga Springs, New York; Arlington, Virginia; and Westminster, Maryland.

The predominant sound was spiky new wave by the likes of the Beakers from Olympia; Seattle's Visible Targets; Portland's Neo Boys; and Get Smart! from Lawrence, Kansas. But it also included excursions into yodeling ("Switzer Boy" by Portland's the Bohemians), experimental jazz ("Men at Work" by the Men, from Chicago), goth (the spooky "Tronada" by Ray Milland of St. Louis), and random weirdness (the bizarre "Slaughterhouse" by All Night Movies from Port Huron, Michigan, which featured various animal grunts).

While most of the acts on the tape would sink back into obscurity (the Beakers had already broken up by the time *Sub Pop 5* was released), some would go on to more renown. Steve Fisk, who would produce Nirvana, Soundgarden, and Screaming Trees, among others, in addition to his own work as a solo artist and the electronic band Pigeonhed, contributed "Digital Alarm," a pulsating track that mixed together percussive sound, keyboards, and spoken word. (He would later join the lineup of Pell Mell, who contributed the surf-rock-meets-new-wave "Spy vs. Spy" to *Sub Pop 5*.) And Jad Fair of the band Half Japanese had yet to launch his solo career when he gave "It Saw Me," a short piece featuring heavily distorted vocals, to *Sub Pop 5*.

Doug Kahn's "Reagan Speaks for Himself" became what Bruce called "the cult hit" of the release. Kahn took an interview by then-presidential candidate Ronald Reagan with journalist Bill Moyers and re-edited it so that the future president was heard delivering such non sequiturs as, "If you open a can of poisoned meat, hold it in your hand, it gets warm very fast, while you're drinking it; we punch the holes in the top and drink it."

"That cut actually got quite a bit of play on college radio because it was so surreal and unique," says Bruce. "And it was definitely the hit of the cassette, even though it wasn't music *per se*. It was very unusual: an alternative spoken-word piece making fun of the president."

Calvin and Bruce also appeared on the cassette, each making their recording debut. Calvin, as a member of the Cool Rays, sang the poppy "Diary of You" in what would become his trademark deadpan, while on "Debbie," Bruce recited a "personal anecdote from my teenage years"—a disturbing story about an encounter with a mentally ill young woman, underscored by an unsettling improvised soundtrack of guitar, bass, and random drum beats.

*Sub Pop 5* had the largest run of any of *Sub Pop*'s cassette zines: two thousand copies, which quickly sold out. Manufacturing costs were $2 per tape, and the cassettes sold for $5, leaving Bruce with a gross profit of $6,000—a tidy sum. "Really good numbers at that time," he agrees. "I think it helped pay my rent for two years."

It also led to Sub Pop's first encounter with the corporate world, when Bruce received a request for a copy of *Sub Pop 5* from Leonard Thompson, East Coast director of talent acquisition at Columbia Records. "I was really kind of flattered," says Bruce. "And it was a smart move; they got access to all those demos for five bucks!" He'd come to feel more conflicted about major-label interest in his projects in the future.

Along with his *Sub Pop 5* appearance, Bruce dabbled in making music, performing with the groups Tiny Holes and War With Elevators. "Olympia in the early '80s had an emerging indie music scene, and I was part of that," he says. "Tiny Holes, which included Steve Fisk on keyboards and synth, was inspired by artists such as Pere Ubu, the Pop Group, and composer Steve Reich. War With Elevators was a spoken-word project, accompanied by beatbox and sax. These were creative projects that helped pass the time while living in a small town."

During this period, he also gained some insight into what life was like on the road for a touring group by joining Portland band Pell Mell on a cross-country tour as a road manager in the summer of 1982. Having to travel two days in a van before they played their first show in Minneapolis brought home to Bruce how isolated the Pacific Northwest music scene was from the rest of the country. But performing was never his primary interest. (In contrast, Calvin Johnson would go on to form the groups Beat Happening, Dub Narcotic Sound System, and Halo Benders, in addition to founding K Records.)

◎ ◎ ◎

In 1982, before moving to Seattle, Bruce put out three more issues of *Sub Pop*. *Sub Pop 6*, published in February 1982, featured the most explicit political statements the zine would ever make. Previous issues had taken swipes at the blandness of mainstream culture, castigating "wealthy biz-execs who sit in air-conditioned penthouses" and railing against commercial music "controlled by an economy based on exploitation and conformity." Now, in a piece about the power of American hardcore, Bruce took aim at a specific target, denouncing President Reagan as "a puppet of the rich."

Calvin went even further, lambasting Reagan as "not a good American. He allows large corporations to run rampant over our environment, huge tax breaks for the rich while stabbing the poor in the back with cuts in social services, and then spends $55 million to kill teenage girls in El Salvador." He was particularly outspoken in arguing that the music scene should be about more than just providing entertainment: "If all an alternative scene does is let you forget about the real world for a couple hours a week, then it's no better than TV, AM radio, or Harlequin romances."

Calvin also advocated getting rid of "the things that hold us back from being truly alternative"—specifically alcohol, calling its consumption "just one way they use to oppress the populace, to funnel your hard-earned money back into the hands of the few." This stance of avoiding intoxicants like alcohol, tobacco, and illegal drugs for political reasons as much as for concern about one's health would evolve into the "straight edge" movement among punk musicians, which was sometimes expanded to include abstinence from caffeine and sex, and adopting a vegetarian or vegan diet.

*Sub Pop 7*, released in the spring of 1982, was another cassette, produced in a run of one thousand copies. There were reappearances by a few acts who'd appeared on *Sub Pop 5* (Get Smart!, Neo Boys, Pell Mell, Sport of Kings from Chicago, Embarrassment from Wichita), with thirteen of the twenty acts hailing from outside the Pacific Northwest, as well as the first non-US act, 50/40, from Surrey, British Columbia.

Overall, it was a stylistic mix, but new wave remained the dominant style, and *Sub Pop 7* revealed how the genre had made inroads across the country. Vibrant Fiasco, who contributed "Lizard Lips," hailed from Aurora, Illinois: "Talk about nowheresville, man, this is about as obscure as we get," the liner notes joked. Zyklon, from Wyoming, Michigan, brought the industrial sounds of another "nowheresville" to vibrant life in "Gary, Indiana" (listeners who were interested in hearing more were invited to write to the band's aptly named label, Grim Records). There was ironic political commentary in Seattle-based Little Bears from Bangkok's ode to consumerism, "Car Buying Time" ("We'll buy a car! We'll buy a steak! We'll buy a baseball glove!"), and there was the poignancy of Bill Legasse, a resident of Boston's Duplex Nursing Home, reciting the story "Worms in It" from a comic book by David Fair (Jad Fair's brother and co-conspirator in Half Japanese).

The *Sub Pop* zines provided a valuable service in sharing information about the range of artists making independent music around the country. They also gave the artists themselves a sense of community: they might be stuck in a regional nowheresville of their own, but they were not alone. And the cassettes heightened excitement in a way that printed materials never could.

"You'd listen to the *Sub Pop* tapes, see what you liked, then go buy the band's record," says Nils Bernstein, then a young music fan in Seattle. "That's the way *Sub Pop* stood out, because other zines didn't provide that. And I remember thinking, 'Man, there is weird shit in these tiny cities!' Now I know that Bruce was trying to highlight things that were outside of New York and LA and Chicago. But at the time I was like, 'Man, there's so much out there!'" It was exactly the kind of reaction Bruce had hoped for.

◎ ◎ ◎

The final print edition of the zine, *Sub Pop 8*, was published in August 1982. Along with such stories as a "US Indie Report," a "Thriftstore 1000" guide to kitschy records found in thrift shops, and a critique of alternative art galleries, there were signposts to the future. Calvin Johnson interviewed the Supreme Cool Beings; the band's drummer, Heather Lewis, would later join Calvin in his first high-profile band, Beat Happening. The zine's third page featured a full-page ad for Triangle Recording, a studio in Seattle; Triangle, under new ownership, would be renamed Reciprocal Recording, and would play a key role in the next iteration of the Sub Pop brand.

By the time *Sub Pop 9* was released the following year, there was a new mailing address, and the "Sub Pop" name was attached to some new ventures. Though his friend Calvin Johnson thought relocating to the big city was "a real sell-out move," Bruce Pavitt had decided to move to Seattle.

## 2
# LAYING THE FOUNDATION

*SUB POP U.S.A. will be a regular column, focusing on a different American city with each issue … Besides local documentation SUB POP U.S.A. will also include a SUB 10 list of local/regional releases from around the country that deserve national/international attention. Please send me free records.*

—Bruce Pavitt, "Sub Pop U.S.A.," *The Rocket*, April 1983

When Bruce Pavitt arrived in Seattle, Washington, in 1983, it was far from the booming tech center it would become in the twenty-first century. The region's largest employer was Boeing, the aircraft manufacturer. Microsoft wouldn't move its headquarters to neighboring Redmond for another three years. Amazon wouldn't open its online doors for another decade.

At the time, the city had no clearly identifiable music scene or regional sound. The club scene was centered on Seattle's historic Pioneer Square district and was dominated by cover bands. In the late '50s and early '60s, a few Northwest acts had found chart success (the Fleetwoods, from Olympia, with "Come Softly to Me" and "Mr. Blue"; the Wailers, from Tacoma, with "Tall Cool One"; the Ventures, also from Tacoma, with "Walk Don't Run"), but there had been no such hit acts in recent years, and musicians from the Northwest generally left town if they wanted to achieve more than just regional success. Heart, from Seattle's suburbs, became popular in the mid-1970s only after moving to Canada; Seattle native Jimi Hendrix didn't become a star until he moved to London.

Nonetheless, there were some in the city who sought out less conventional entertainment. Though all-ages venues were typically short-lived, new spaces continually popped up, and the *Sub Pop* zines helped publicize them while they existed. The *Seattle Syndrome* and *Seattle Syndrome Two* compilations, released in 1981 and 1982, respectively, showcased acts that had no interest in becoming cover bands, such as the power-pop Fastbacks (whose drummer, Duff McKagan, would soon head for Los Angeles and become the bassist in Guns N' Roses), the post-punk Blackouts (whose members would later resurface in Ministry), and the sarcastic Mr. Epp and the Calculations—two of whose members would go on to be in the longest-running band ever to be on Sub Pop.

Small though it was, the music scene was large enough to support a music magazine, *The Rocket* (which went bi-weekly in 1992 and folded in 2000). The magazine covered touring acts but gave plenty of coverage to local music as well; the calendar listings and the free musicians available/musicians wanted classifieds made it a must-read for anyone who was interested in what was happening musically in Seattle.

Bruce, who'd graduated from Evergreen in 1981, had stayed in Olympia for a while, "living a post-college, bohemian lifestyle, staying creative while doing part-time gigs to get the bills paid." But as work became harder to find, he decided to move north, to Seattle. He remained as committed as ever to the idea of establishing a music scene of one's own. When Duff McKagan, who worked alongside Bruce in the kitchen of Seattle's Lake Union Café, announced that he was moving to Los Angeles to become a rock star, Bruce asked why he didn't just work at becoming a rock star in Seattle. "There's no way you can make any money playing music in Seattle," Duff told him. In less than five years, McKagan would be riding high with Guns N' Roses. "He proved his point," Bruce later conceded. "But at the same time, the vision that I was carrying [was] that if you actually stayed where you lived ... you could do the same thing."

Bruce quickly set about establishing himself as a presence in his new home. He met with Bob Newman, the editor of *The Rocket*, and persuaded him that what the magazine needed was a column that focused on independent releases. Thus "Sub Pop U.S.A." made its debut in *The Rocket*'s April 1983 issue. The first column featured a brief write up of *Seattle Syndrome Two* ("Face it, few cities could put out a pop compilation this good"), but Seattle acts rarely rated a mention in "Sub Pop U.S.A." during its first year, with the exception of Mr. Epp's breakup being noted in the March 1984 column.

"So many acts were reviewed right as their first records were coming out," says Bruce. "For example, the Beastie Boys, or Run-DMC, or Sonic Youth—a lot of acts that went on to become culturally really significant. And because I was so focused on new indie stuff, I was able to kind of nail it on a wide variety of acts."

The Sub Pop brand—and Bruce was already thinking of it as a brand—next expanded to the airwaves, when *Sub Pop U.S.A.* became the name of Bruce's radio show on KCMU-FM, the radio station affiliated with the University of Washington (UW). He also served as the DJ for a short-lived all-ages club in Pioneer Square called the Metropolis. Local acts such as the U-Men, the Visible Targets, and the Fastbacks were excited to get the chance to share the stage with out-of-towners such as the Replacements, Violent Femmes, Bad Brains, and John Cale. (Mark Arm was amazed when Mr. Epp and the Calculations were paid $100 for a show they played at the club.)

Bruce's day jobs were also in the music industry. He worked for a while at a shop called the Record Library, which had a novel concept of renting out records to customers, and later landed a job there for fellow Evergreen student Russ

Battaglia. When the business was shut down due to complaints from record companies that feared the shop was encouraging home taping, Bruce and Russ opened their own shop, Bombshelter Records (a precursor to a later venture, Fallout Records & Skateboards, which would open in July 1984).

Bruce's final cassette zine, *Sub Pop 9*, was released in June 1983, in a run of five hundred copies. Most of the twenty-three featured artists (including Bruce, whose pieces "Random American Television" and "Random Swedish Radio" opened each side) were from outside the Pacific Northwest, including two songs by nameless bands from behind the Iron Curtain: "Due to diplomatic promises on my part, no address or info can be given," Bruce wrote in the liner notes. Some old friends returned: the tape featured the jaunty electric pulsations of "Love Is" by Steve Fisk; the minimalist, vaguely unsettling "To the Beach" by Heather [Lewis], Calvin [Johnson], and Laura [Carter]; and what Bruce called the "sweet, soulful electronic dub workout" of "Chain of Abuse" by John Foster's Pop Philosophers.

Another friend from Olympia, Rich Jensen, contributed the edgy spoken-word piece "No Cannibals on This Cul-De-Sac." Rich had taken a keen interest in Bruce's activities since being introduced to him by Calvin Johnson. "They were part of this local gang of people making culture and moving the ball right in this tiny little town where I was," he says. "It was really exciting, and I did what I could to make them want me to join their gang. It wasn't even that what we were doing would ever reach anywhere. But it was clear that something was building."

*Sub Pop 9*'s liner notes had urged, "Remember: buy local, think global, but order it from SUB/POP." But Bruce's next project put the name on hold. In 1984, he released the first record by the U-Men, a Seattle band whose dark, punky spin on garage rock made them the top alternative act in town at the time. But instead of releasing the band's self-titled four-song EP on Sub Pop, Bruce elected to release it on a new label, Bombshelter, which he named after his record shop.

"At the time, Bombshelter seemed a more established business," he explains. It was an unexpected detour. But it wouldn't be too long before the Sub Pop name was revived once again.

◎ ◎ ◎

By 1985, Bruce had left Fallout for Yesco Audio Environments, a company that created background music for businesses (later better known by the name Muzak, which bought out Yesco in 1987). His somewhat lofty title of "tape returns coordinator" masked a more prosaic reality: he was responsible for duplicating tapes and cleaning tape cartridges. But the pay and benefits, including health insurance, were welcome ("My appendix surgery was well timed," he jokes), and, more unexpectedly, he found himself among a group of fellow music fans and aspiring musicians, including Mark Arm (later of Green River and Mudhoney), Tad Doyle (TAD), Grant Eckman (the Walkabouts), and Chris Pew (Swallow), all of whom would later record for Sub Pop. "It helped to solidify the scene," says Bruce, "in that you had a group of people who were working together side by side, every day, for months at a time, and developing a certain camaraderie, a certain trust, a certain understanding of each other."

In 1986, Bruce released another Sub Pop compilation, but this time on vinyl, not cassette. "It developed organically out of the fanzine," he says. "I was writing about a lot of music that people really had a hard time getting access to, so releasing cassettes with songs from some of these groups seemed to make sense. And once the tapes started doing fairly well, transitioning to vinyl was pretty easy. Everything just flowed from wanting to share music with people."

Instead of continuing the series with *Sub Pop 10*, Bruce conveyed a real sense of taking the label in a fresh direction by naming this latest release *Sub Pop 100*. The cover featured a jagged illustration by Northwest artist Carl Smool, depicting a young couple grinning (or grimacing) as they fire their weapons. On the spine was the inscription, "The new thing: the big thing: the God thing: a mighty multinational entertainment conglomerate based in the Pacific Northwest." It was a typically bold claim for a label whose "office" consisted of a post office box.

"I wanted to release a trans-regional compilation, like the tapes, in vinyl form," Bruce explains. "Sonic Youth gave me the go ahead to use 'Kill Yr Idols,' so I felt that it would be successful." *Sub Pop 100* had a heavier, rawer sound in comparison to the new wave influence evident on the Sub Pop cassettes. The bands were part of the new generation of indie-rock acts: not only Sonic Youth but also Scratch Acid (from Austin), Naked Raygun (from Chicago), and Skinny Puppy (from Vancouver, BC). There were nods to the Northwest via the inclusion of tracks by the U-Men and Steve Fisk. The album opened with a heavily distorted spoken "introduction" by Steve Albini, who was then in the industrial punk-rock band Big Black, but closed in lighter fashion, with the kitsch pop of Japanese band Shonen Knife (followed by a short excerpt from a Barry White song).

The record's cover and label also featured the debut of the Sub Pop logo. The heading for Bruce's *Rocket* column, designed by Wes Anderson, appeared as a banner, with "SUB/POP" on top and "U.S.A." underneath. For *Sub Pop 100*, Dale Yarger (another *Rocket* designer) cut the "U.S.A." and stacked "SUB" and "POP" on top of each other. Carets (sideways arrows) placed between the "U" and "O" provided a bit of additional space. The logo that would go on to grace countless T-shirts—among other items—was born.

Rich Jensen, who'd moved to Seattle, offered his house for *Sub Pop 100*'s release party. The record sold out its five-thousand-copy run, enabling Bruce to take a vacation in Amsterdam. Promoting the compilation also brought him into further contact with another young man who was working to establish himself in the Seattle music scene: Jonathan Poneman.

Jon, like Bruce, was born in 1959. He grew up in Toledo, Ohio. "Quite ironically, when I was very young, I was incredibly sensitive to loud noise," he says (a condition caused by the underdevelopment of myelin, a protective substance on the nerve endings, in his system). He nonetheless went on to develop a keen interest in music, and, again like Bruce, remembered being thrilled by a song at a social function, in this case Steppenwolf's "Magic Carpet Ride," which he heard at a cousin's bar mitzvah when he was ten years old. "Suddenly, this crazy sound unlike anything I had ever experienced happens over the stereo," he told *Pitchfork*. "It kind of frightened me at first, and then it began to get really loud, and then it suddenly kicked into a song. I loved it."

From then on, he was all in. In 1975, he and a friend hitchhiked from their school in Bloomfield Hills, Michigan, to see Bruce Springsteen in Detroit, waiting for hours so they could secure seats in the front row. (Jon was awestruck when the Boss jumped off the stage and into his friend's lap during "Rosalita.") He also learned the power of music to provoke; when he played Led Zeppelin's "Moby Dick" for his classmates during show-and-tell, his teacher quickly took the needle off the record before it could finish.

His family moved to Phoenix, Arizona, and, after graduating from high school, he moved to Bellingham, Washington, with his girlfriend. By now, he'd discovered punk and new wave (Television's *Marquee Moon* was a record he "worshipped") but knew few people who shared his interests; when he stopped by the local music store, Discount Records, in search of the Clash's debut album, "The guy behind the counter was pooh-poohing it, then going, 'Now, this Gerry Rafferty record ....' That kind of summed up Bellingham for me."

He'd found a punk scene in Vancouver, BC, only fifty-four miles from Bellingham, and considered moving there when he and his girlfriend broke up in 1979. But the difficulties in sorting out the legalities of moving to another country made Seattle an easier option. "I came down here and did every dead-end, menial job that a person could do," he says. At least the music scene was more to his liking: "Two days after I moved to Seattle, I saw Magazine, the Blackouts, and Dr. Albert play at the Showbox. That was a great show!"

He also had his own ambitions. "My primary motivation was to get in a position in the music community where I would not be invisible," he says. He was in two new wave bands, the Rockefellers and the Treeclimbers, though more for fun than as a serious pursuit. And he began moving in the same circles as Bruce, stopping in at Bombshelter Records and running into him at KCMU, where Jon had taken over the program *Audioasis*, which showcased local bands. (The show still runs on KCMU's successor station, KEXP.) For his part, Bruce recalled Jon visiting a friend at Yesco (Jon having also worked at the company), intrigued to see that he was carrying a record by the rapper Schoolly D.

When *Sub Pop 100* was released, Jon interviewed Bruce for *Audioasis*. "It was during that interview that we really got to know each other," says Bruce. "Jon was thoughtful, and obviously a true music fan." Jon later admitted to being initially intimidated by Bruce's reputation. The *Audioasis* interview changed his perception. "Bruce is a really sensitive person, and I dialed into that pretty quickly as soon as I actually met him," he says. "A very funny, smart, very clever social observer and self-marketer. He was a dynamic and charismatic guy." He also recognized Bruce's underlying motivations. "Bruce was a mover and shaker. And, like so many of us, he was looking for the next step to take to get out of menial work. And trying to figure out how to champion and make a living simultaneously out of the things he believed in and was excited about."

There was another compilation released in 1986, one that focused exclusively on the Pacific Northwest: *Deep Six*, the first release from Seattle-based C/Z Records. C/Z was started by Chris Hanzsek and his then-girlfriend Tina Casale, the name taken from letters in their last names. Hanzsek had been living in Boston, trying to break into the music industry, and decided to move to a city that didn't have as much of an established scene. He chose Seattle after a friend sent him the *Seattle Syndrome* compilations.

In January 1984, Hanzsek and Casale opened Reciprocal Recording in Seattle's Interbay neighborhood, but they lost the lease after a year. While looking for a new space, they began work on *Deep Six*, the record with which they planned to launch C/Z Records. The idea for the compilation came from Seattle band Green River, who recorded their first demo at Reciprocal. Along with Green River, *Deep Six* also featured tracks by Soundgarden and Skin Yard (both from Seattle), Malfunkshun (from Bainbridge Island, Washington), and the Melvins (from Montesano and Aberdeen, Washington). The U-Men were also added to the lineup to enhance the package; they were the only group who'd previously released a record.

The album's official release date was April 1, 1986 (the band members had received their copies in February 1986). "I think *Deep Six* did its job in the sense that it was a signal flare that there was something afoot, that there was life on this planet here in Seattle," Hanzsek told author Mark Yarm. "*Deep Six* is the best testament—a snapshot before things got out of control," says Daniel House, Skin Yard's bassist.

The bands didn't all sound alike, but their common influences meant they shared a similar perspective. "We all had something in common in that we all knew each other, and we'd all played shows with each other," says Jack Endino, Skin Yard's guitarist. "There was a small music scene; there were only a couple of clubs, and it seemed like wherever I went it was the same bands playing in the same clubs with the same audience. There were other little music scenes in town; the early '80s new wave scene was still hanging in a little bit, but a lot of that had faded by 1985. We sort of had our own thing."

A common factor was the blending of punk and heavy metal, two genres that had previously been regarded as warring camps. The new bands weren't as rigid about the punk/metal divide, having grown up listening to Led Zeppelin, Aerosmith, KISS, and Black Sabbath, and not leaving them behind when they moved on to the Ramones, the Sex Pistols, and the Clash. Journalist Dawn Anderson understood this when her review of *Deep Six* for *The Rocket* described the songs as "music that isn't punk-metal but a third sound distinct from either."

Bruce naturally wrote about *Deep Six* in his "Sub Pop U.S.A." column: "It's SLOW and heavy HEAVY and it's *the* predominant sound of underground Seattle in '86 … [the bands] prove that you don't have to live in the suburbs and have a low IQ to do some *serious* headbanging." He was especially taken with Green River. Green River had come together in 1984 from the remnants of Seattle-area bands Mr. Epp and the Calculations (Mark Arm, guitar), the Limp Richards (Steve Turner, guitar), Spluii Numa (Alex Vincent, drums), and Deranged Diction, originally from Montana (Jeff Ament, bass). When Mark decided to focus on singing, another friend, Stone Gossard (who'd played with Steve in yet another band, the Ducky Boys), was brought in on guitar. The name was an example of the black humor espoused by Northwest bands, referring not to the Creedence Clearwater Revival song but to a local serial killer, so-named because the bodies of his first victims were found in the Green River, located just outside Seattle. (The killer, Gary Ridgway, would finally be arrested in 2001.)

Mark nonetheless cites Creedence as an early influence for Green River, along with the Stooges, Alice Cooper, and Tacoma, Washington, garage rockers the Sonics. To their surprise, they were soon fielding offers from three different record companies. After sharing a bill with Green River, Tom Flynn, guitarist with Los Angeles–based punk act Fang, offered to sign them his own label, Boner, while demos that Jeff Ament sent out attracted the attention of Enigma. "Enigma sent us a sixty-four-page contract that scared the shit out of us," says Mark. "Boner at that point was just the label that Fang owned; it seemed a little less established."

Homestead Records was also interested, Bruce (not yet ready to throw his own hat into the ring) having tipped off the label's owner, Gerald Cosley, about the band. And with a roster that included alternative acts such as Nick Cave, Foetus, and Sonic Youth, not to mention Seattle's U-Men, it seemed the logical choice. Green River released a six-song EP, *Come on Down*, on the label in 1985 and went on tour to promote it, playing a handful of dates, including a closing spot at CBGB on a Wednesday night. "We played cleanup, essentially," says Mark. "We basically played to the bar staff."

It didn't help that the EP had not yet been released while the band was on the road. "The record stiffed and the band got dropped," says Bruce. "But I still thought they were a brilliant band, especially live." Green River next released the single "Together We'll Never"/ "Ain't Nothing to Do" on their own Tasque Force label (a play on the name of the Green River Task Force, set up to catch the serial killer). As a favor, Bruce included copies of the single when he mailed out *Sub Pop 100*. Now he determined that Sub Pop would release the next Green River record.

The band began work on *Dry as a Bone* (a five-song EP) in July 1986, at the new Reciprocal Recording. Chris Hanzsek had learned from Jack Endino that Triangle Recording (whose control room had been featured on the cover of *The*

*Rocket*'s debut issue) was closing, and the two took over the lease. (Though they had initially formed a partnership, Jack ultimately decided he didn't want to deal with the business side, and Hanzsek bought out his interest.) Reciprocal would become the go-to studio for Sub Pop's early acts, who would also end up working with the same producer: Jack Endino.

Jack was born in Connecticut and had moved to Bainbridge Island as a teenager. He graduated from the University of Washington in 1980 with a degree in electrical engineering, then spent the next few years working as a civilian engineer at the Puget Sound Naval Shipyard in Bremerton. Tiring of the of the day-to-day grind, he quit and moved to the small town of Belfair, Washington, where he taught himself to play guitar and drums and learned the basics of recording.

After moving back to Seattle in 1984, Jack became friends with Daniel House, and the two formed Skin Yard. He was also recording bands in his basement, and had already worked with Soundgarden and Green River (he'd mixed the latter's Tasque Force single).

Reciprocal, he recalls, was "a terrible studio. Terrible acoustics, and a control room that was much, much too small. But I had no way of knowing that at the time. And if someone knows what they're doing, they can make a good recording anywhere, and I'd been making perfectly good recordings in my basement on my 4-track machine. So it wasn't very hard to make good recordings in a place that seemed rather palatial, actually, compared to my basement.

"At Reciprocal, I had a real recording room, isolation, headphones and good microphones, some speakers and a mixing board, and a good 8-track machine. It was all good equipment. It's just in the sense in which I know a studio now, I realize it was a terrible little place. But I had nothing to compare with. And it was inexpensive—it was cheap. I could afford to record bands there. There was no other studio I was ready to work in."

As Jack didn't feel he had enough studio experience, he hesitated to call himself a producer; his work on Sub Pop's early records had the credit "recorded by." But Bruce felt Jack's records had their own distinctive sound. "All my favorite bands were recording with Jack," he says. "His recording style effectively captured the rawness of the bands while keeping costs radically low. Jack—along with the photographs by Charles Peterson—created the vibe that put Seattle on the map. He is a wizard."

It took Bruce over a year to release *Dry as a Bone*; he only managed to get it out after receiving a loan from his father. (Jeff Ament said the band also had to put up money for the record's release.) The record was finally issued in July 1987 and was Sub Pop's first non-compilation release. It was also the first to feature photos by Charles Peterson.

Charles, who grew up in the Seattle suburb of Bothell, had met Mark Arm at the UW and had previously taken pictures of Mark's band Mr. Epp. Like Mark and Bruce, he was also a DJ at KCMU; his own show followed Bruce's. It was Mark who suggested that Bruce check out Charles's work.

Charles's black-and-white photos captured the visceral excitement of a rock show and the energy generated by the interplay between audience and performer. "I really wanted to portray *that*, versus just the singer at the microphone nonsense," he says. "I was using this blur, and quite often not even looking through the camera when I took pictures, getting weird angles, and just trying to get in there as much as possible. There's almost this shamanic quality to some of the photos; the band's all blurry and the audience is all blurry, and they're all coming together, and the band's jumping on the audience and the audience is jumping on the band, and it's such a release. That's what I wanted to portray."

Bruce was captivated with Charles's pictures, especially as they reflected his own ideas about the wealth of undiscovered music you could find in regional scenes. "At the time, we wanted to make the bands look a little bit larger than life," says Charles. "That was the appeal to people living elsewhere: 'Oh, look at this band, and the audience is going crazy!' When if you panned the camera over this way, you'd notice that really there's only twenty-five people in the club. You wanted to make it look like, 'Wow, Seattle is really going off!'"

Charles would become Sub Pop's go-to photographer, just as Jack Endino was the go-to producer. Using the same photographer's work on Sub Pop's early releases helped create a uniform look; Bruce wanted a potential record buyer to be able to identify a Sub Pop record by its look as well as its sound. And, hoping to create the greatest impact, he opted to release EPs as 12-inch records, giving him a larger sleeve to display the artwork. "We were fans of the EP format," he explains. "I always felt that EPs made a better impression."

Sub Pop's promotion of *Dry as a Bone* also included a word that finally gave a name to the punk/metal hybrid sound of the new bands, with the label's catalog describing the record as "ultra-loose GRUNGE that destroyed the morals of a generation."

"It just seemed appropriate," says Bruce. "I don't think the word was really being used at the time, but it seemed very appropriate." Mark Arm had actually been the first person to use the word "grunge" to describe Seattle music when, as a joke, he wrote a letter to a short-lived Seattle music publication called *Desperate Times* in 1981 that brazenly attacked his own band: "I hate Mr. Epp and the Calculations! Pure grunge! Pure noise! Pure shit!" He signed the letter with his real name, Mark McLaughlin.

◎ ◎ ◎

*Dry as a Bone* wasn't the only record Sub Pop released in July 1987; there was also a single by Soundgarden, "Hunted Down"/ "Nothing to Say." Bruce's roots with Soundgarden went back to his days in Illinois; Kim Thayil, Soundgarden's guitarist, and Hiro Yamamoto, the band's bassist at the time, had been in the same ALPS program with him. Kim was also friends with one of Bruce's younger brothers and had been in a local band, Identity Crisis, with another Pavitt brother. Since moving to Washington, Bruce had been mailing records to Kim, who became intrigued enough (especially by the music of the Blackouts and the Beakers) that he himself moved to Seattle in 1981, bringing Hiro along for the ride. Kim enrolled in the UW, and he soon had his own radio show on KCMU.

In 1984, Hiro began jamming with Matt Dentino, another Park Forest friend. The two formed the Shemps, with Kim occasionally sitting in. A *Rocket* "musicians wanted" ad looking for a vocalist and a drummer was answered by Chris Cornell, who ended up taking on both duties. Then, after Dentino's departure, Hiro and Chris persuaded Kim to join the band full time. They took the name Soundgarden from the name of a sound sculpture in a local park called "A Sound Garden," enjoying the dichotomy of giving a hard-rock band a gentle-sounding name. It quickly became apparent that singing was Chris's real strength, so he was moved out from behind the kit. Scott Sundquist was the band's drummer through the recording of *Deep Six*, after which Skin Yard drummer Matt Cameron replaced him.

In addition to his other ventures, Jon Poneman booked local acts at the Rainbow, a club in the University District. He first saw Soundgarden at the club in 1985. "They completely blew my mind," he recalls. It was also the moment he realized his own musical abilities would never make the grade, "because this was a band that effortlessly inhabited, *possessed*, the qualities of rock 'n' roll that I always thought were important; an element of spontaneity, danger, intensity. Their *effortlessness*, really." After the band's set, he promptly approached Cornell, offering his services to help the band in any way that he could.

Bruce had also been following what his high school friends were up to. He'd heard an early demo of the band, and, like Jon, was similarly "blown away" by their music. "Soundgarden had a very unique blending of commercial and alternative sensibilities," he later observed. "You had a singer who was a classic rock star, sang like Robert Plant, looked good, and you had a guitar player that listened to a lot of underground music and would experiment with atonality as well as heavy riffing; it's not the kind of guitar playing you would expect to hear in a commercial metal band. Plus, because they had really slowed the tempo down and were very bass heavy, they had a super heavy sound that was not necessarily commercial at the time. It was basically Led Zeppelin meets the Butthole Surfers." He also liked the band's ethnic mix, with two Caucasian members, Kim having Indian heritage, and Hiro being Japanese: "That really went counter to a lot of corporate LA commercial hard rock, which was almost uniformly white males."

Jon desperately wanted to work with Soundgarden. He considered starting his own record label but wasn't sure how to go about it. He also viewed Bruce as a potential rival. One day, on walking into the Oxford Tavern, a bar in downtown Seattle, he saw Bruce sitting at a table with Soundgarden and immediately became nonplussed. "I thought, 'Here is Bruce Pavitt, muscling in on my turf.'"

After learning that Bruce wanted to release an EP with Soundgarden on one side and Seattle band Feast on the other, Jon contacted Kim Thayil. "Are you really going to do that?" he asked. "Well, we're thinking about doing something," Kim replied. "But you know, Jonathan, you should really think about working with Bruce. Because these ideas that you've been having, he's got the same ideas. And I think you two would get along really well."

"Jonathan was very confident in his own ability to get a record out there and have people notice it," Kim explains. "We weren't as confident. We knew he could make a record, but we knew that Bruce could get it noticed."

Sub Pop was an established label, but there was little capital. As Bruce put it, "My assets included an answering machine and a roll of stamps." Jon lacked experience but was willing to find money to invest. He agreed to raise $2,000 for the recording of Soundgarden's first EP, *Screaming Life*, by borrowing the money from family and friends.

"Hunted Down" and "Nothing to Say," the first two songs from the *Screaming Life* sessions, were released on blue vinyl in a limited-edition run of five hundred copies; the single was also sent out with promo copies of *Dry as a Bone*. But though "Hunted Down" was the A-side, it was "Nothing to Say" that pointed the way to Seattle's musical future.

It was the first song Kim had written using drop-D tuning—tuning the low E-string down a whole step. The Melvins had used drop-D tuning in their songs, Buzz Osborne having picked it up from Larry Kallenbach, a friend of Melvins drummer Dale Crover. Buzz in turn mentioned the tuning to Kim and Mark Arm, pointing out it was used on songs like Black Sabbath's "Into the Void." "And we were all like, 'Really?'" Kim told *Guitar World*. "All I knew of altered tunings back then was slide guitar tunings, like what the country guys used …. I wrote the song 'Nothing to Say,' and Chris wrote 'Beyond the Wheel,' and we became married to that tuning."

The drop-D tuning gave the songs a darker feel, a minor-key dissonance that tugged at the heartstrings. It was also a sign of a definite Seattle *sound* coming into its own. Leighton Beezer, a member of numerous Seattle bands, offers a humorous demonstration of what grunge is in the 1996 documentary *Hype!*, first playing a riff from the Ramones' "Rockaway Beach" on his guitar and identifying it as punk rock. He then plays a riff from Green River's "Come on Down," before stating triumphantly, "And that's grunge!" The word was not in common usage yet, but the style had been laid down.

Jack, who'd recorded the tracks, knew they'd done something special with "Nothing to Say." "We thought, 'Man! Listen to this thing, this sounds crazy!'" he recalls. "It sounded good and we were happy about it. I was really excited as well, like, 'This is only an 8-track recording, but it sounds enormous.' I was doing good work, considering the technical limitations that I had. But sometimes limitations of money or time or equipment mean you have to actually get something done, because this is all you've got. And some amazing records, some amazing artistic statements have come out of those limitations at times."

Following the release of *Screaming Life* in October 1987, Bruce asked Jon if he'd be interested in investing money for Sub Pop's next venture, Green River's *Rehab Doll* EP. Jon jumped at the opportunity. He'd hosted the release party for *Dry as a Bone* at another club where he did bookings, Scoundrel's Lair, and had been dazzled by the band. "I had seen them many times previously, but I'd always written them off as kind of a joke band," he says. "This was the first time where I saw them and they were commanding. It was this communal experience, just bathed in glorious, mind-shattering rock. And I was completely mesmerized. Had I not seen that show, I would've been, 'Well ….' But after that show—I had seen some good Green River shows, but this was like a whole different thing. So I said, 'Hell yes!'"

As Bruce and Jon talked, they realized they were both interested in promoting more of the music they found in their own backyard. "Starting with *Dry as a Bone*, I definitely wanted to focus on what was happening in Seattle," says Bruce. "Focus on the Northwest, be a Northwest record label, the same as Motown was a Detroit label." Jon's investment would cover more than just Green River; he put up $19,000 for a 50 percent share in Sub Pop ($14,000 from his savings and another $5,000 from his brother). "And so, with that, it was like, 'We're gonna do it!'" says Jon. Bruce and Jon were now officially partners.

◎ ◎ ◎

On January 23, 1988, a three-piece act from Aberdeen, Washington, made their way to Reciprocal Recording. Jack Endino had taken a call from a young man whose name he heard as "Kurt Covain," who wanted to record some songs. What made Jack take notice was that Kurt said one of the musicians accompanying him would be the Melvins' Dale Crover. Skin Yard had played shows with the Melvins, and Jack had been impressed by Dale's prowess, which made him look more favorably on his new clients. "That meant it's not going to be some shitty band, if Dale's with him," he says.

Kurt (Cobain, not "Covain," Jack learned) turned up with Dale and a lanky, six-foot-seven bassist named Krist Novoselic. The group, which had no name, arrived at noon and worked quickly, knocking out ten songs in four hours, then spent another two hours on mixing. Before the trio left for Tacoma, where they were booked to play a show that evening, Jack gave them a quick cassette dub of the session and asked if they'd let him keep the quarter-inch 8-track master so he could dub another copy for himself.

"If I liked something, I often made myself my own copy," he explains. "Kurt's singing stood out, because he was really pretty impassioned, and some of the songs were pretty good. It sounded as good as any of the Seattle bands that were getting all the hype at that point."

The musicians agreed, saying they'd pick up the master tape later. It was a decision that would lead to unimagined consequences.

# 3
# THE GRUNGE YEARS

*For Sub Pop, 1988 was a year of many firsts: our first office, our first employee, our first bounced check(s)—and that was just April!*

—Jon Poneman, Sub Pop catalog description for *Sub Pop 1000*, 2013

When Bruce sat down to write his first "Sub Pop U.S.A." column of 1988, he was eager to promote the thriving creativity he saw around him. "1987: Hey, did it suck or what?" he observed, in a column entitled "27 Reasons Why Washington State Is a Cool Place to Live." "Maybe for the rest of the country, but not around here. 1987 was easily the best year for local music since Bing Crosby rocked Tacoma. And that was back in '38."

"By '87 and '88, I was really convinced that the Seattle music scene was an incredibly happening music scene," he says. "I was going to a lot of shows, I was seeing the stuff first hand, I was starting to release some of these records. And when you go through that list [in the column], it doesn't even have Nirvana on it, you know? No Nirvana, but Screaming Trees, Soundgarden, TAD, the Fastbacks, Girl Trouble, the U-Men, Young Fresh Fellows, the Melvins—this is amazing stuff. So many of these bands went on to have cult followings or really helped to influence culture. And again, this is before Mudhoney or Nirvana, the two bands that really helped blow up the scene."

Despite Bruce's optimistic boosterism, Sub Pop was actually on shaky ground as 1988 dawned. Soundgarden would release one more record on Sub Pop, but they had already signed a one-album deal with Los Angeles–based SST

Records. "It was disappointing but understandable," says Bruce. "SST was very influential at the time."

And, to Bruce and Jon's further dismay, they'd lost another valuable asset when Green River broke up in late 1987. After Steve Turner's departure from the group, a schism in the remaining members' musical interests had developed; Jeff Ament and Stone Gossard wanted to pursue a more commercial direction, while Mark Arm favored a raw, indie-rock style. The band had nonetheless continued working on *Rehab Doll*, but the final night of their 1987 West Coast tour brought Green River to a sudden end.

On October 24, the group had opened for Jane's Addiction at a Los Angeles club called the Scream. Jeff had put several A&R reps on the band's guest list, to Mark's dismay; he'd wanted to invite more friends. Only one rep showed up, too late to catch the band's set, which was perhaps just as well, as Mark had blown out his voice at the previous night's show in San Francisco. And while Jeff and Stone were excited by Jane's Addiction, who'd drawn a crowd of two thousand without even having a record deal, Mark was unimpressed; it was obvious the musicians were no longer compatible. Back in Seattle, when Mark and Alex Vincent arrived for a practice session on Halloween, Jeff, Stone, and Bruce told them they were out of the band.

Mark quickly rebounded. That same evening, he ran into Dan Peters, the drummer in Seattle band Bundle of Hiss, at the OK Hotel, and told him the news. In short order, Mark, Dan, and Steve Turner were soon jamming together; they then found a bassist in Matt Lukin, who'd been kicked out of the Melvins (Buzz Osborne and Dale Crover had told Matt they were breaking up the band, then moved to San Francisco and started it up again without him). The new band took their name from a Russ Meyer film that had recently played on a Meyer triple bill at Seattle's Neptune Theatre: Mudhoney

Mark brought in the band's demos to play to his co-workers at Muzak. Bruce quickly recognized the band's potential and sent them into the studio. "Mudhoney is the band that really launched Sub Pop," he later said. "Sub Pop would not exist without Mudhoney, would not have happened without Mudhoney … they were absolutely brilliant immediately, so it was our good fortune, our good grace to have this amazing band come together right as we were trying to launch the label."

That view was confirmed when the band played their first show on April 19 at a Seattle club called the Vogue. "It was just astounding," Bruce recalled. "They were brilliant … and their live shows were very spontaneous, very physical, very funny. They really epitomized the spirit of Sub Pop, which really had a lot to do with humor—humor in rock 'n' roll. They were definitely the flagship band there for quite a while."

By then, Bruce and Jon had seen another band they'd soon add to Sub Pop's roster: the band whose demo Jack Endino had recorded in January '88, who were now calling themselves Nirvana. Jack had made copies of the band's demo and passed one to Jon, who immediately fell in love with the first song, "If You Must." (Ironically, Kurt Cobain disliked the song, and the band soon dropped it from their set list.) Bruce felt otherwise, having played the tape at Muzak, where it received a less-than-enthusiastic response: "The general consensus was that Kurt was a good singer, but the material really wasn't very good." He was no more convinced when he and Jon caught a sparsely attended show at Seattle's Central Tavern, feeling the group had no stage presence. He agreed to release a single, but insisted it had to be the band's cover of "Love Buzz," originally recorded by Dutch act Shocking Blue (best known for their 1969 hit "Venus"), as he didn't think Nirvana's original material was strong enough.

In March, Bruce and Jon took a big step and quit their day jobs. Sub Pop had acquired its first office, in the penthouse of the Terminal Sales Building, at 1932 First Avenue in downtown Seattle, for a rental fee of $200 a month. "It was a bold move," says Bruce. "It's when we really started to go into it professionally. Even though we weren't necessarily that professional in our execution, it was a pretty big leap for us. It sure felt good to quit my job at Muzak. It was a blessing that we both had really crappy jobs!" They formally took over the lease on April 1, 1988; henceforth, April Fools' Day would be designated as Sub Pop's official anniversary date.

Though being in the "penthouse" sounded glamorous, the reality was more mundane. The elevator stopped at the tenth floor, meaning you had to walk up a flight of stairs to actually reach the office. And the space was hardly palatial; in lieu of storage rooms, record stock had to be stashed in the bathroom.

Being in business full time was more challenging than Bruce and Jon realized. By the beginning of May, they'd gone through most of their money, leaving them unable to pay the printing bill for the *Rehab Doll* sleeve. Bruce persuaded the printer to give them the sleeves on credit: "If he didn't advance us the sleeves, the printer would be stuck with them, as we wouldn't be able to pay until we actually sold some of the records."

The company's motto, "Going out of business since 1988," was meant as a joke, but it was rooted in truth. "In the early days, it was barely managed chaos," remembers Daniel House. Skin Yard's bassist had just quit his day job at a printing shop, and, on the way home, had ended up giving a lift to Jon, whom he'd seen waiting at a bus stop. On learning that Sub Pop was looking for someone to handle sales, he quickly offered his services.

"Things were growing at a rate that Bruce and Jon themselves could barely keep up with it," he continues. "They were really bad with money and they were pretty fucking disorganized. They were always kind of scattered between too many things, and weren't particularly good at time management. But they were also the cat with nineteen lives. It amazed me how they could make some of the biggest blunders and it would just turn around and somehow benefit them." Sub Pop's ability to weather innumerable storms yet somehow land upright would serve them in good stead in years to come.

Charles Peterson, who'd been hired as Sub Pop's receptionist, among other duties, also found the first months to be "pretty tenuous. Especially when payday came around, and whoever was first in line at the bank could maybe cash their checks. I remember I handed out the envelopes with the checks, and would be like, 'See you guys!' and run down to the bank and get first in line."

"I think there was a long period when they were just trying to figure out what this was going to be," says Nils Bernstein, the music fan who had picked up the Sub Pop cassettes and was now running his own record shop in Seattle, Rebellious Jukebox. "It was this kind of incremental thing. They'd put out one record, you didn't know if there would be another record. And it was singles without picture sleeves; it was as bare bones as it could be—they were given away at shows! The early mythology around Sub Pop was that from the very beginning, they said, 'These are amazing bands, and you're missing out if you're not on board!' and made it out to be this massive scene. But then, like positive new age affirmations, it turned out to be true."

For his part, Bruce hoped an esprit de corps would develop at the burgeoning company, despite the business difficulties. "When you're working together, when you're running a mom-and-pop business, which is what Sub Pop was, it's essentially an extended family," he says. "Half the time you can pay your bills, half the time you can't, and the only thing that's going to keep you together is just a sense of trust and camaraderie, and an underlying understanding that we value this culture and we're all just going to do whatever it takes to make it happen."

"As cliché as it is, there was that kind of Mickey Rooney, 'Hey, let's put on a show!' kind of thing," says Charles. "We all just wanted to do it, just to do it. It wasn't this moneymaking operation at all."

If Sub Pop didn't have much capital, the company did have something else: an established brand. And Bruce realized you didn't need to have a lot of money to enhance that. He'd noted that labels like UK-based Factory and 4AD had cultivated a specific look and sound, which he didn't see happening among stateside indie labels. While working at Bombshelter and Fallout, he'd seen customers buying records simply because they were on a particular label. He wanted to generate the same kind of excitement about Sub Pop's releases. "There was a real emphasis on giving focus to the graphics, and maintaining a certain uniformity with the sound through the production of Jack Endino," he says. "I thought that was key as far as establishing a label identity."

Appealing to collectors was another strategy, with limited-edition runs of releases on colored vinyl. The first six hundred copies of Soundgarden's *Screaming Life* EP were on orange vinyl; the first eight hundred copies of Blood Circus's first single came on red vinyl; the first six hundred copies of Swallow's first single came on yellow vinyl. A determined collector would have to acquire all of them.

Bruce and Jon were also keen to get Sub Pop's name out there in any way possible. "There were a lot of labels or artists who wouldn't think of doing an interview for the Costco newsletter, but we would do that," said Bruce. "We had this philosophy that we would never turn down an interview for any reason or anybody. We wanted the name Sub Pop to just permeate the culture."

Humor was also a key factor. Sub Pop's promotional efforts were decidedly tongue-in-cheek, parodying the corporate culture the label's co-founders had just escaped from at Muzak. In their imaginations, Sub Pop wasn't a business struggling to keep its doors open, but a multinational corporation on its way to what Bruce and Jon were sure would be "World Domination."

"I was writing the ad copy for Sub Pop, with a hype style that was coming into practice towards the end of my 'Sub Pop' column," Bruce explains. "Jon and I both shared a self-deprecating sense of humor, as did Mark Arm. I think we all felt that the punk scene was taking itself too seriously at the time, so we approached the label with a sense of the ridiculous." Bruce's business card gave him the title of "Corporate Magnate." Jon's read "Corporate Lackey."

The iconic "LOSER" T-shirt allowed the label's fans to join in on the fun. "I remember saying we needed to have a Sub Pop shirt with 'LOSER' emblazoned on the front and the Sub Pop logo in back," says Bruce. "It was brought to my attention recently that Mudhoney manager Bob Whittaker used to wear a T-shirt with 'Loser' on it, so give credit to Bob. As with any culture, ideas are traded back and forth. The bold black lettering of 'LOSER' complemented the logo, and was part of the vibe."

Bruce and Jon were also pleased at the message the shirt sent during a decade so devoted to conspicuous consumption. "It was a real anti-yuppie statement," Jon proudly told the *Seattle Post-Intelligencer.*

This freewheeling spirit was evident in the company's other business dealings as well. Like many small labels, Sub Pop often had difficulties being paid promptly by the companies that distributed its records. In July 1988, while attending the New Music Seminar, a music industry event in New York City, Bruce and Jon dropped in at the offices of one of their distributors, Caroline Records, wearing T-shirts bearing the inscription "YOU OWE ME MONEY." "We never brought up the bill once the entire time," Bruce recalled. "And by the time we left, they handed us a big fat check."

Beneath the humor was an unwavering faith in their product. "I did sincerely feel the Seattle scene was going to blow up—but not to the degree it did," says Bruce. "I was thinking about the impact that Detroit had in the late '60s, early '70s, with the Stooges and MC5. I felt we were on a similar trajectory."

Just three months after Sub Pop officially opened its doors, Bruce received confirmation that they really were on to something. A music fan from Brooklyn, Ed McGinley, called Sub Pop's offices and ended up talking to Jon about records. Jon happened to mention that there was a great show coming up: Soundgarden, Mudhoney, and the Fluid were playing the Central Tavern on July 2. "And this guy got on a Greyhound bus and traveled three thousand miles for this show!" Bruce marvels. "I tell people that that was the moment where I realized—this scene is about to blow up. If people are willing to get on a bus and travel three thousand miles for a show, they're getting it. They're realizing that there is something happening here that isn't happening in other parts of the country."

July also marked the end of an era for Bruce; it was the final appearance of his "Sub Pop" column (the "U.S.A." had been dropped in July 1987). "I was writing about my favorite bands, then I started putting out records by my favorite bands, then I started reviewing the records that I was putting out by my favorite bands," says Bruce. "And it was just getting a little too much of a conflict of interest."

The final column was mostly devoted to Bruce asking his friends, "What's Hot and What Sucks?" In a closing fillip, Jon, identified as a "sleazy record executive," cited "Madagascar cuisine" as "hot," while saying that the Sub Pop column "sucks."

◎ ◎ ◎

It took time to get Sub Pop up and running. The first release of 1988 was Green River's *Rehab Doll*, with the initial one thousand copies pressed on green vinyl. There was also Soundgarden's *Fopp* EP, which featured two versions of the title track (a cover of the Ohio Players song) and a cover of Green River's "Swallow

My Pride," as well as releases by Mudhoney, Tacoma's Girl Trouble (a joint release with K Records), and TAD. Aside from *Clear Black Paper* by Denver act the Fluid (first five hundred copies on blue vinyl), it was a completely Northwest roster.

"Sub Pop effectively had two different marketing strategies," says Bruce. "One, put a media focus on Seattle by releasing records by—mostly—Seattle bands, and two, network with different scenes by releasing a relentless schedule of singles by out-of-town bands. This was an outgrowth of the Sub Pop cassettes, which succeeded by reaching out to different scenes, connecting with different markets." Through his zine and column, Bruce already had numerous contacts among independent labels in other cities, and he kept an eye on what was happening outside of Seattle. He'd learned about the Fluid through a friend, and as Sub Pop's bands began to tour, they were encouraged to pass on tips about interesting bands they discovered.

For now, though, Northwest acts took priority. "With regards to the Northwest, I had this vision of Washington State being like an island, okay?" Bruce later explained. "And in the same way that the UK is an island and created music that influenced the world, and in the same way that Jamaica is an island that created music that influenced the whole world, I started to see Washington State as an island. And I felt that if we could really generate communication between the different scenes, that we could as well create music that would influence the rest of the world."

To help maintain a steady cash flow, an innovative system of selling stock to record shops directly, thus bypassing a distributor, was devised. "My basic task was to establish and build and grow the whole direct-to-retail network of stores that became very much the bread and butter of the label for the longest time, in terms of keeping the lights on," says Daniel House. "What was unique about this was there were other labels that sold records to stores. But everything was returns—thirty-day, sixty-day. Sub Pop's model was different. Sub Pop was COD; nobody had ever done that before."

"It was hard at first," he admits about getting stores to go along with such a system. "But Sub Pop got pretty major press pretty early on. And with early releases like Soundgarden and Green River, it was a kind of a big deal out of the gate pretty quickly."

Sub Pop also began distributing releases by other independent labels, like K Records. "Part of the reason for distributing other product was there wasn't enough Sub Pop product a lot of the time to warrant a full sale," Daniel explains. "But when we had other stuff to make it worthwhile, people started jumping on board. So I started dealing with lots of record labels and overseas distributors. We were distributing exclusively for Waterfront [based in Australia], and we were importing a lot of stuff from Glitterhouse [based in Germany]. We wouldn't distribute entire labels. I was very, very picky and choosy. The whole thing was curated. And so it started to become kind of a big deal, if you could get Sub Pop to distribute your stuff. We became tastemakers in that regard. Inside of about a year, I had established and was the sole salesman for over two hundred accounts, nationwide."

But Sub Pop continued to use distributors for its own records as well, which occasionally led to conflict. "I was effectively creating competition," Daniel says. "Our distributor, Caroline, hated it. They were like, 'You're undercutting us!' And my response was like, 'You know, you have an entire company. I'm one person. If you are doing a good enough job with our stuff and getting our product where it needs to be, stores will buy it from you. Albeit at a slightly higher price, but they're not paying cash. And we keep hearing all these stories of stores that are getting short shipped; they'll order ten copies of Mudhoney and they get three. So what this says is that you're not ordering enough of our product. And they order from us and they get their orders filled; if they order five, they get five.' That actually created an incentive for them to work harder to sell Sub Pop product."

Another revenue stream came from the creation of a series aimed directly at collectors: the Sub Pop Singles Club. As with a magazine subscription, the buyer paid upfront to receive a year's worth of limited edition singles made exclusively for the club, without knowing what they were going to be. "We're ripping you off big time with our Sub Pop Singles Club," the label's catalog bragged.

The first Singles Club release was Nirvana's "Love Buzz"/ "Big Cheese," issued in a run of one thousand copies in November 1988. Kurt Cobain later revealed "Big Cheese" was a subtle commentary on his feelings about Jon Poneman being "so judgmental about what we were recording"—ironic, given that it was Bruce who was less convinced about signing the group.

The limited-edition strategy quickly paid off, and during its first run, the Singles Club would have a peak of forty-five hundred subscribers ("Love Buzz" would later draw bids in excess of $3,000 at auctions). It even attracted the attention of the major labels. In 1990, Don Ienner, then president of Columbia Records, told Bruce he was amazed that Sub Pop could get people to send in money for records before knowing what they were going to be. Bruce explained that they played to a collector's mentality: because the releases were limited editions, paying in advance was the only way to ensure that you'd get one.

A similar flair for marketing was shown with *Sub Pop 200*, a compilation released in December 1988. Though the set's twenty recordings could have easily fit on two albums, it was decided that releasing the tracks on three EPs, adding a twelve-page booklet, and packing everything in a boxed set limited to five thousand copies would have a greater impact.

In typically grandiose fashion, the booklet's first page had a photo of the Terminal Sales Building, identified as "Sub Pop World Headquarters." The same page included pictures of key staff. Bruce and Jon wore identical suits and ties, with Bruce listed as "Supervisory Chairman of Executive Management" and Jon as "Executive Chairman of Supervisory Management." The picture of Charles Peterson depicted him wearing the "YOU OWE ME MONEY" T-shirt. The accompanying copy read, in part, "We at Sub Pop take great pride in offering you the finest in Northwest ROCK. Remember, if it isn't Sub Pop, it probably sucks."

"It was just overkill—sheer overkill and maximum hype," Bruce later told *Rolling Stone*. The booklet's cover art, by Charles Burns, showed a sinewy guitarist walking through a garbage heap of broken records and audio equipment; in an unfortunate note of prescience, the guitarist has a monkey strapped to his back.

The twenty tracks on *Sub Pop 200* fully justified Bruce's view of the Northwest having an "incredibly happening" music scene (the Fluid, again, was the token non-Northwest act). There was the taut power of the opening track, TAD's "Sex God Missy"; the garage rockabilly of Girl Trouble's "Gonna Find a Cave"; the pop leanings of Nirvana's "Spank Thru"; a fuzz-drenched cover of Jimi Hendrix's "Love or Confusion" by Screaming Trees (from Ellensburg, Washington). There were unexpected forays into folk-rock (the Walkabouts' "Got No Chains"—Sub Pop's catalog called them "Sensitive hippies with big amps"), singer-songwriter acoustics (Terry Lee Hale's "Dead Is Dead"), and spoken word (the gnarly voice of Jesse Bernstein working his way through "Come Out Tonight"). And there was humor: Soundgarden returned to drop "Sub Pop Rock City" (which featured a few answering machine sound bites from Bruce and Jon); *Seattle Syndrome* veterans the Fastbacks took Green River's "Swallow My Pride" for a spin; and Mudhoney turned in a droning number that turned out to be a cover of Bette Midler's "The Rose."

"To me, *Sub Pop 200* felt like a turning point," says Charles Peterson. "Here was this fairly elaborate package for the time, and all these bands, and I felt like, okay, here we have this pretty serious foundation of talent. And if each one of these bands puts out a record, a full record, you've got a roster. You've got a label."

Aiming to spread the word as far as possible, Bruce and Jon asked Norman Batley, a British expat who worked as a DJ in Seattle, if he would send a copy of *Sub Pop 200* to one of his London contacts, John Peel, who hosted an influential show on BBC Radio 1. It paid off handsomely, with Peel not only playing the record on his program but also writing a favorable review in the *Observer*—the first substantial piece written about Sub Pop overseas. It added to the growing momentum; in 1989, Sub Pop would go international.

◎ ◎ ◎

Mudhoney's first single had been released in August 1988 (the first eight hundred copies on brown vinyl), featuring the track that would become the first classic anthem released on Sub Pop, as well as Mudhoney's signature song: "Touch Me I'm Sick." From the jagged guitar intro to Mark's howling of the song's title, the track was a clear descendant of proto-punk Northwest acts like the Sonics, whose garage-rock classics included the likes of "The Witch" and "Psycho."

Now off to a roaring start, Mudhoney became the first Sub Pop act to perform overseas, playing the Berlin Independence Days music festival on October 10, 1988. That appearance got them a European booking agent, who arranged for the band to open for Sonic Youth on their upcoming European tour.

In advance of the tour, Anton Brookes, a publicist for London's Southern Record Distributors (which distributed Sub Pop's records overseas), suggested that Sub Pop fly over a writer and photographer in exchange for a cover story in the UK weekly *Melody Maker*. Bruce and Jon readily agreed; this played right into their penchant for hype. Everett True was the chosen writer, and Bruce and Jon wanted to make sure that by the time he left Seattle, he'd been dazzled by everything that Sub Pop had to offer.

"That whole thing was orchestrated—and very well orchestrated, I might add," says Daniel. "They set up all of these shows ahead of time, specifically for his visit, to give Everett a very specific impression—that Sub Pop bands were playing every single night. But that wasn't the reality most of the time. Yeah, sure, all those bands were playing around with regularity, but it wasn't like every one of the bands on the roster was playing night after night at these different clubs. It was a brilliant bit of manipulation. And it paid off. It paid off in spades."

True rose to the occasion. "Britain is currently held in thrall by a *rock* explosion emanating from one small, insignificant, West Coast American city," he wrote in his Mudhoney cover story, which appeared in *Melody Maker*'s March 11 issue, going on to laud the group as a "four-headed long-haired ferocious noise pop beast, reared on a diet of the Sonics and the Stooges, King Crimson and Minor Threat." The story ended with Mark Arm's puckish quote, "We say fuck the kids! Except the kids who buy our records. Then they're fucking themselves." The following week, there was another two-page spread on Seattle bands in the magazine, with True calling Sub Pop the "life force to the most vibrant, kicking music scene encompassed in one city for at least ten years."

Bruce had been making similar statements in his "Sub Pop U.S.A." columns, but seeing such claims boldly proclaimed in a magazine like *Melody Maker* gave the label a new credibility. The British music weeklies (there were four at the time) were all in fierce competition to discover the next big thing. True's coverage instantly drew the attention of the rest of the UK music press to Sub

Pop and its bands, who came to be viewed as stars in the making—despite the fact that most of the groups had rarely played outside of Washington State.

Similarly, Sub Pop played up the supposed provincialism of its bands, knowing that would play well in a foreign market. True's articles, for example, referred to Mudhoney as "working class," even though two of the members had been to college, while Tad Doyle was described as being from "the backwoods of Idaho," and the members of Blood Circus were summed up as "complete and utter white trash."

"We all resented Sub Pop to an extent for that," says Kurt Danielson, TAD's bassist. "But on the other hand, we understood it as a necessary promotional gimmick, a gimmick that seemed to work. What you want is to have people at your shows and buying your records; if these things accomplish that, then so much the better."

Sub Pop's profile was further heightened stateside at the label's first "Lame Fest," held on June 9 at Seattle's Moore Theatre, featuring Nirvana, TAD, and Mudhoney and billed as "Seattle's lamest bands in a one-night orgy of sweat and insanity!" Initially, there had been doubts that the show would make any money; local bands played clubs, not a fifteen-hundred-seat theater. But the concert ended up selling out.

"Booking the Moore was an epic gesture, which is how we did things," Bruce notes with pride. "The bands were killing it live, so we knew Seattle would go off if we could get people there. The theater's manager let most of his security staff go prior to the show, thinking that nobody would show up. And there was complete pandemonium. Google those YouTube videos, kids, it's an epic moment!" The show doubled as a release party for Nirvana's first album, *Bleach* (the first thousand copies on white vinyl).

Nirvana had also recently become the first act to sign a record contract with Sub Pop. Earlier in the year, Nirvana bassist Krist Novoselic had turned up at

Bruce's house one evening, demanding a written contract; previously, Sub Pop had only made verbal agreements with its artists. Jon hastily drafted a one-year contract, with options for two further years; the contract was signed on June 3 but backdated to January 1, 1989. "Righteous heaviness from these Olympia pop stars," was the Sub Pop catalog's assessment of *Bleach*. "They're young, they own their own van, and they're going to make us rich!"

The success of the first Lame Fest led to a second one being held overseas. "Jon and I had very little resources but a lot of enthusiasm at that time," Bruce recalls. "And we were constantly brainstorming and trying to piece together strategies that would help convince the rest of the world that Seattle had an amazing rock scene. Once we saw that model work in Seattle, we were really dead set on getting all three bands playing in London and getting as many press people and photographers there as possible."

With Nirvana, TAD, and Mudhoney all touring the UK and Europe that fall, a Lame Fest date was arranged for December 3 at London's Astoria Theatre. Bruce cites the concert as "a true turning point in the international stature of the Seattle music scene." He made sure to take pictures during the show (later published in his book *Experiencing Nirvana: Grunge in Europe, 1989*). "Almost every live shot has people jumping off the stage," he points out. "The show rocked. Everybody was ecstatic, and you can see it in the response from the audience."

It wasn't just rock audiences. Major labels were now paying attention to Sub Pop as well, and the company began fielding calls from executives interested in setting up some kind of business arrangement with the company. "The most significant conversations were with Columbia," says Bruce. "We had a full staff meeting with them around May 1990. I'm very glad that that did not unfold. Jon was the corporate liaison of sorts, and kept the door open for conversations. I did not feel comfortable with it, but I was open to see what could be negotiated."

One unintended effect of meeting with major labels was that they didn't come without costs—legal fees. "There were some legal expenses, which hurt our situation," Bruce concedes. And as Seattle's music scene grew hotter, Sub Pop found it was not only attracting major label interest but having to compete with major labels as well. Soundgarden, having recorded an album for SST, swiftly moved on to A&M. Following Green River's demise, Jeff Ament, Stone Gossard, and Bruce Fairweather had formed Mother Love Bone, who landed a deal with Polygram (though the band came to a tragic end when lead singer Andy Wood died of drug-related causes on March 19, 1990). Other bands were also fielding offers. "We needed to have additional resources if we wanted to keep playing on the same turf that we were playing on," says Jon.

To keep artists from leaving, they were asked to sign new contracts; in turn, the bands demanded higher advances. Nirvana balked at re-signing with Sub Pop and decided they'd rather deal with a major label directly, sending out the songs they'd recorded for their second Sub Pop album to land a deal of their own. When rumors of Nirvana's upcoming defection reached Sub Pop, Bruce went to Kurt Cobain's home to plead his case, noting that both of them championed outsiders and underdogs—a perspective Kurt was unlikely to encounter among those working at a major label. "And he agreed," says Bruce. "But I think the financial incentives outweighed the hipster cred I had at the time. In retrospect, it's understandable that the band moved on, but at the time, I took it personally."

Nonetheless, the label still appeared to be going from strength to strength. Megan Jasper, Sub Pop's receptionist, who'd grown up in Worcester, Massachusetts, and landed at the company after falling in love with Seattle while working as a roadie for Dinosaur Jr., painted a vivid portrait of life at Sub Pop World Headquarters in an interview for the Museum of Pop Culture's oral history archive:

There was such an incredible element of creativity at the label. In one room you'd have Bruce sitting on the floor trying to put an advertisement or a poster together, then you'd have Jonathan going through cassette after cassette after cassette listening to new stuff. Bruce might start dancing any minute, you never knew. Erica, who did all of the promotions, would start shooting her mouth off, and God knows what was going to come out, but it was probably something that was not pretty. It was exciting and it was fun and it was really great to be a part of.

Jonathan would come in around 10, 10:30, and we'd usually go out and get coffee and baked goods; there was a lot of coffee and baked goods going on, eventually I think we all ended up being baked goods ourselves in more ways than one, but Bruce would come in around 11 and there was always a major shift when those two came in the office. It was all of us catching up before they came in, and then all of the sudden it was like trying to keep up after that. But it was great. It was really fun to work there.

Jon told the *Seattle Times* that he estimated Sub Pop would gross over a million dollars in 1990. In the liner notes for a compilation of Seattle bands called *Fuck Me I'm Rich*, a co-release with Waterfront Records, the two moguls bragged about their good fortune. "If anybody tells you that they play rock music for any other reason than to make millions and millions of dollars— they're lying," wrote Jon. "But while you're buying the implied importance of rock music, I'm buying houses, cars, villas on the Costa Del Sol! That's rock 'n' roll!" Bruce was equally jocular, writing, "Now, as I gaze at the unfortunate below, I realize that my penthouse view is the result of honest work & impeccable media exploitation. Cough. As a God, I have nowhere to go but down."

◉ ◉ ◉

But pride cometh before a fall. Despite the boasting, Sub Pop's financial situation was becoming increasingly precarious. In 1991, the label landed in serious legal trouble over the artwork for TAD's *8-Way Santa* and the accompanying single, "Jack Pepsi." The album cover featured a picture (found in a photo album picked up at a thrift store), of a smiling young man and woman, the man's hand planted on the woman's bikini-covered breast. The woman, who'd since divorced the man in the photo, was now a born-again Christian, and was horrified when she saw the album cover. She took legal action, and the record was quickly withdrawn and reissued with a new cover. (Copies of the original cover immediately started selling for $50.)

As for "Jack Pepsi," an anonymous interviewee in Greg Prato's *Grunge Is Dead* claimed that a "disgruntled Sub Pop employee" who'd been fired had tipped off Pepsi-Cola to the fact that the single's artwork parodied the soda pop logo; the company was also displeased that the lyrics were about driving drunk after consuming the titular beverage combo (Jack Daniels and Pepsi). That single also had to be withdrawn and reissued in a new cover, with the track itself renamed as, simply, "Jack."

The fact that the company hadn't been keeping close track of its funds added to its difficulties. "There were a couple of checks that bounced," says Jack Endino. "Sub Pop eventually paid; they always came up with the money. But sometimes there would be a few panicky phone calls: 'Wait, wait, we'll have you paid next week.' And they always came through. But they did bounce a couple of checks, it must be pointed out."

Bruce admitted the company didn't always avail themselves of a professional bookkeeper: "Ironically, we were trying to save money!" By 1991, he says, "All of our six distributors owed us money. And we had a distributor in Canada that folded, owing us $40,000, which was a huge amount for us at the time."

In a sign of things to come, Daniel House was fired in January 1991, having been told by Bruce, "Your band and your label seem to be taking more of your attention." Daniel disputed this claim. He pointed out that he had already quit Skin Yard, and, while he was also running a record label of his own, having taken over C/Z Records from Chris Hanzsek, he maintained that he never worked on C/Z business on Sub Pop's time.

There had been tension between the two nonetheless, as Daniel felt Bruce had never liked his band. Angered by what he felt was an unflattering description of Skin Yard's "Start at the Top" single in the Sub Pop catalog, he'd released a C/Z T-shirt with the phrase "BRUCE PAVITT GAVE ME HEAD" written in a style that parodied Sub Pop's logo. "I think at first Bruce was a little miffed, because it was a direct slap back at him, personally," Daniel admits. "But it was also a riff on Sub Pop—so, indirectly, it was another way to give attention to Sub Pop."

Daniel suspected he was really being fired because his salary was deemed too high. And certainly, later in 1991, there were layoffs to cut back on costs. As the staff shrank from twenty-five to five, Megan Jasper was among those who lost her job. Record releases were delayed due to problems with the vinyl manufacturers, further hindering the label's cash flow. Sub Pop negotiated an exclusive deal with Caroline in exchange for a modest advance, but it wasn't enough to ease the company's dire financial straits. It was a period Bruce remembered as being "excruciating." Gallows humor resulted in the production of a T-shirt that read, "What Part Of WE DON'T HAVE ANY MONEY Don't You Understand?" It was a joke, but there was an uncomfortable truth underneath: Sub Pop was running on fumes.

# 4
# GRUNGE GOES SUPERNOVA

*1992 was the year the international attention was focused longingly on you, the denizens of the fabled Grunge Rock Scene. You wore flannel and kids in Tokyo swooned. You forgot to wash your hair and fashion models stopped bathing altogether. You said mosh and Madonna took you out to dinner to ask how high.*

—Seattle club RKCNDY's monthly calendar, January 1993

Bruce looked drawn and tired on the August 1991 cover of *The Rocket*. His mood was explained by the adjoining headline: "Sub Plop? Is the price of world domination too high?" The story depicted a company whose offices had become "chaotic beyond all reason."

"They had lots of money and they blew it," Daniel House was quoted as saying. "They just spent it on everything, everywhere, every way they could."

Bruce and Jon were interviewed for the article too. Jon, while agreeing that their business acumen left something to be desired, had no regrets for having indulged in "grandiose gestures" over the years: "If we had been fiscally more restrained we probably wouldn't have gotten a tenth of the hype." He also insisted things were better than they appeared: "We have been cleaning up the mess piece by piece, step by step."

A similarly themed but more critical piece, "Is Sub Pop About to Pop?" ran in the *Seattle Weekly* on October 23. "Idealistic in philosophy, self-described as naïve in market practices, Bruce and Jonathan have gained a reputation as difficult—sometimes incompetent—business partners," author Glen Hirschberg wrote. Geoff Kirk, a former bookkeeper at Sub Pop, was quoted as saying he'd warned the company repeatedly about the dire financial straits they were in, to no avail. He learned he was fired when he arrived at the office and found that his key no longer worked. "We didn't handle a whole lot of things well," Jon admitted in the story. But he continued to insist things were improving at the label. And indeed, by the time the *Seattle Weekly* article ran, things were looking up. But it hadn't been easy getting there.

In May 1991, when Bruce's Olympia friend Rich Jensen learned there was a bookkeeping position open at Sub Pop, he contacted Bruce, who asked him to come in for an interview. Rich prepared himself by immediately heading to the library and checking out a copy of Barbara Gilder Quint's *Clear and Simple Guide to Bookkeeping* to get a crash course in accounting. At the interview, Bruce asked him about his experience. "And I go, 'Well, I worked in the business office for the School of Dentistry at the UW,'" Rich recalls. "And that was good enough for him."

Rich was brought into "this little disorderly room full of paper" and put to work right away. "The first thing I did was figure out which pieces of paper had dollar signs on them, and put those in a stack. Then go through those, and look at who they were from and whether they were money in or money out, and what the date was. I put all those into an Excel spreadsheet. Took a couple days. I printed it all out; it was this long dot matrix print out that was about eight feet long, and it had a sum at the bottom. And I taped this eight-foot long dot matrix print out with all the different people that were owed money in Bruce's window across from his desk. And in big bold letters at the bottom it said $200,000. And I know at that moment there was five thousand dollars in the bank.

"It was an interesting time," he continues, with some understatement. "Bruce and Jon were so busy; it's very taxing emotionally to have responsibility for people and not know how you're going to get through that period. There was also a lot of tension around some of the artists; it had been quite a bit of time since there had been a royalty statement. There was very little money to pay anyone, but it was also unclear what might be owed, and that's a scary thing for both parties. I was pretty good with the numbers. I found a $60,000 error in one of the distributor statements. And Bruce said, 'You earned your pay today!' And that certainly helped things."

It also helped that Rich didn't immediately give up his other job as a bus driver, and that he had some savings, "so I didn't need to be paid right away. I just believed so much in what was going on there that I was able to come in and put things together."

Once Rich had sorted out the figures, he was able to work out payment plans. "There would be money coming in. So I was able to put a budget together as to how the rent could be paid, and people could get their fractional payments of bills owed, and the phones would stay on, and the van wouldn't be repossessed, and the county tax authority wouldn't close the door—which were all about to happen by July. And it worked out."

Mudhoney provided another reprieve. Given Sub Pop's financial turmoil, the band had been deliberating about whether they'd release their next album, *Every Good Boy Deserves Fudge*, on the label. Sub Pop owed Mudhoney money too; when Steve Turner dropped by the office saying Jon had promised him a check, Bruce gave a nervous laugh in response. (When the two talked about the matter the next day, Bruce broke down in tears.) Being offered stock in Sub Pop instead of the cash caused the band members to break into laughter themselves. But to Sub Pop's relief, Mudhoney decided to go ahead with the release. *Every Good Boy Deserves Fudge* came out in July 1991 and immediately jumped into the UK charts, peaking at no. 37 and going on to sell over seventy-five thousand copies worldwide. "This was like getting a gold record in the punk rock world," Bruce observes.

Then came the release of Nirvana's *Nevermind* on September 24. DGC Records had bought out the band's contract with Sub Pop for a very welcome $75,000; the label would also get a 2 percent royalty on the band's next two DGC albums. In early sales meetings, DGC projected that *Nevermind* would sell around fifty thousand copies. But there was a buzz about Nirvana, and after witnessing the excitement the band's shows generated, Mark Kates, DGC's head of promotion, dreamed that sales might reach half a million. Even that proved to be wildly underestimated; five weeks after its release, *Nevermind* had breezed past that mark, on its way to selling over thirty million copies worldwide. Then, on January 11, 1992, it hit no. 1 on the *Billboard* charts, eclipsing Michael Jackson's *Dangerous*. Alternative rock had conquered the mainstream.

It was a windfall. Sales of *Bleach* began to climb; the album eventually sold over a million and a half copies, making it Sub Pop's biggest seller to this day. More money came in with the release of *Incesticide*, a 1992 compilation that featured material from Nirvana's Sub Pop years, and Nirvana's *In Utero* album, released in 1993. "We went from the walking dead to totally rocking," says Bruce. For the first time in Sub Pop's history, the company had no pressing financial worries.

◎ ◎ ◎

Nirvana's success was followed in short order by other Seattle-based bands: Pearl Jam (Jeff Ament and Stone Gossard's new band after Mother Love Bone imploded), Soundgarden, and hard rock outfit Alice in Chains. Overnight, the Seattle music scene became the center of the rock music universe, and the music industry rushed to catch up. The 1990 album *Temple of the Dog*, a tribute to Mother Love Bone lead singer Andy Wood, had initially been released to general indifference. Now it was heavily promoted as an album featuring the members of Soundgarden and Pearl Jam, reaching no. 5 in the US and selling over a million copies. Cameron Crowe's romantic comedy *Singles*, set in Seattle, had been stuck in limbo after completion, with the film studio unsure of how to promote it. Now, when the studio realized the film featured songs and performances by the likes of Alice in Chains, Pearl Jam, and Soundgarden, it was quickly released, along with an accompanying soundtrack, which reached no. 6 in the US and sold over two million copies.

For Bruce, this was a transformational moment. He draws a parallel with Nirvana's own experiences touring Germany in November 1989, when the borders between East and West Germany were opened for the first time since the construction of the Berlin Wall. "It was fascinating to hear Nirvana's response to that epic historical moment," he says. "And I feel in some ways there's a metaphor, or analogy. When Nirvana knocked Michael Jackson off the top spot on the *Billboard* charts, to some people coming from the indie rock–punk rock scene, that felt like the fall of the Berlin Wall. To me, there was kind of an echo of a revolutionary moment, like, 'Oh my God, I never, ever, ever thought I would see the day that the Berlin Wall would come down'—or that an underground band that did shows with Sonic Youth and the Butthole Surfers would knock not just anybody off the pop charts, but the King of Pop. So that had a revolutionary feeling to it."

"It was a heady time, it was a perplexing time, it was a fun time," says Jon. "Probably as a good a time to spend one's youth as any. On some level, it didn't surprise me when these bands became popular. Because as a fan, I thought they should be popular. But in the real world, stuff like that rarely seemed to happen. And so that it actually happened with our friends, in our community, right before our eyes seemed miraculous."

Media attention focused on more than just music. There were features touting a perceived Northwest "lifestyle," revolving around Gen X kids who bought their clothes at thrift shops, drank coffee at one of Seattle's many espresso bars by day, and indulged heavily in local micro-brewed beer by night. "Jolted by java and looped with liquor, no wonder the music sounds like it does," Michael Azerrad wrote in *Rolling Stone*.

Bruce viewed this as an extension of the kind of hype Sub Pop had been indulging in for years—though without the irony. "I was always thoroughly entertained by every moment of it," he said. "It never got too strange for me. I thought it was just incredible …. Grunge fashion down the runway and Sears Roebuck grunge-wear, and grunge pencil sets with [Seattle-based cartoonist] Peter Bagge on the front. It was endlessly amusing to me. I was laughing the entire time, loving it."

Being natural pranksters, they even enjoyed playing along with the hype. Jon obligingly provided the copy for a fashion spread in *Vogue*'s December 1992 issue, "Grunge & Glory," writing, with tongue firmly in cheek, "I had moved to Washington from Ohio in the late seventies filled with less-than-great notions, a would-be guinea pig for designer antidepressants. Like many of my peers, I chose not to battle the encroaching ennui. Instead, I let it consume my life. The soggy Northwest climate only damped my ambition, which makes it all the more amazing that I stumbled onto such a mother lode of inspiration." Jon hadn't turned in the copy in a timely fashion, and ended up having to hurriedly write it while on a business trip in Vermont with Bruce. "I literally freehand wrote that thing in the back of Joyce's car," he says. (Joyce was Joyce Linehan, who would later run Sub Pop's Boston office.) "I read it once a few years ago, and I went, 'Oh, Jesus.' But just know that it was written under duress!"

In the accompanying photo spread, *Vogue* described the grunge look as "an all-American street fashion that mixes rough-and-tumble work clothes with waifish thrift-shop finery"—though it's unlikely the $760 Calvin Klein Collection dress worn by one of the models ever turned up in any thrift shop.

Mudhoney's wry response was the song "Overblown," which appeared on the *Singles* soundtrack. Seattle musician Sara DeBell, unintentionally referencing Bruce and Jon's past, recorded easy-listening, Muzak-style renditions of "Touch Me I'm Sick," "Swallow My Pride," and "Smells Like Teen Spirit" for her album *Grunge Lite* (released on C/Z). "*Grunge Lite* creates a relaxing mood, bringing sparkle and magic to your dinner parties and tranquilized moments at home," read the liner notes.

But the cleverest prank was Megan Jasper's. After being laid off by Sub Pop, she took a job with Caroline Records. She was at home when she received a call from the *New York Times*' Rick Marin, looking for grunge slang terms to include in a sidebar to a grunge-themed story he was writing. He'd initially asked Jon for help, but Jon referred him to Megan, knowing she would have more fun with the request. Megan suggested Marin give her a phrase and she would tell him the "grunge equivalent."

"So I'm giving him these fake things; weird things that come to mind, or funny stupid terms I used with some of my skateboard friends," Megan recalls. An uncool person, Marin was told, was a "lamestain"; a person with a domineering significant other was "bound and hagged."

Marin soaked it all up. "Then I started to get a little bit bored," says Megan. "And so I tried to get more ridiculous so that he would go, 'Oh my God, you're kidding me.' But that just didn't happen." Even "Swinging on the Flippety Flop"—supposedly slang for hanging out—didn't provoke a response. "And that was one of the ones where I thought, all right, he's going to laugh and I can say, 'You know, there isn't really a secret language or slang.'" Instead, "Lexicon of Grunge: Breaking the Code" ran as a sidebar to Marin's story "Grunge: Success for the Great Unwashed," which appeared in the *Times* on September 16, 1992. Daniel House quickly printed up T-shirts with either "lamestain" or "harsh realm" on the front, and the C/Z logo and the "Lexicon" sidebar on the back.

That none of the bands that captured the most attention were actually on Sub Pop anymore was a minor point; simply being the label that helped launch Nirvana, Soundgarden, and (indirectly) Pearl Jam provided enough cachet. "The press wanted quotes for their Nirvana story or whatever," says Nils Bernstein, the owner of the Rebellious Jukebox record store who had been hired by Sub Pop to do retail promotion in 1991 and later moved to publicity. "But my actual job was doing publicity for Sub Pop's artists. And so you're in a position where you're trying to promote lesser-known bands and just trying to use the label's reputation to hope that people will pay attention. And people did, because it was Sub Pop. People still wanted to take my calls. They were curious as to what Sub Pop was doing, and they wanted access to Sub Pop in general. People wanted to be part of what was going on in Seattle, so they wanted to be friends with people at Sub Pop. It was a company that people wanted to be a part of. And it was fun."

As a longtime music fan, Nils felt the "real peak" had come when Soundgarden and Screaming Trees signed to SST. "That was just like, man!" he says. "That was amazing. So everything after that just seemed crazy. Like the movie *Singles* was a real shark jump, I think. I remember Ron Reagan [President Ronald Reagan's son] came to do a story for *60 Minutes* or something, and I was like, 'Why am I hanging out with Ronald Reagan junior?' Things like that just seemed ridiculous. Not good or bad, just ridiculous. It all just became weird and funny. It's kind of that thing where it's such a small, personal scene for so long, and you know that you all have the same kind of cultural and musical references. Then it becomes quite big, and it became a lot of people going to shows that you had nothing in common with, you didn't have any common musical references. And that felt weird. It started to not feel like ours anymore."

"The relentless media attention was both a blessing and curse," says Bruce. "I remember Jon and I doing some kind of interview every day, with post-*Nevermind* '92 most likely being the peak. One day it would be a Spanish TV crew, the next it would be *Time* magazine, and so forth. But we had a policy of never turning down an interview, as it was crucial to building the brand."

◉ ◉ ◉

But it was one thing to talk about "World Domination" and another to have to actually deal with it. "Is it possible to become commercially successful without co-opting your values?" Bruce had wondered to the *Seattle Times* in 1989. "I don't know. The odds are totally against it. But that's what we're trying to do."

Now that Sub Pop was financially successful, its position had altered. "As kings of the hill, now we are the things to beat," Jonathan said at the end of 1992, to the local music publication *Hype*. "We are yesterday's news. How do we collectively redefine ourselves? Or do we? Do we just keep on being who we are, and who we've always been?"

To Jon, there was a new degree of exploitation in the local scene, with other labels rushing to Seattle looking for the next Nirvana. "For us, it doesn't make it fresh anymore," he told *Hype*. "We want to be in areas where there is still an element of excitement." He also admitted to being burned out on rock, especially as Sub Pop was now being inundated with demos, "which were all fifth-rate Mudhoney clones."

Accordingly, Sub Pop broadened its palate to a greater degree than ever before. There were certainly releases that could qualify as "grunge" among the forty-two records the label released in 1992: records by Love Battery and the Mark Arm/Steve Turner side project the Monkeywrench, as well as offerings from Northwest acts such as the Fastbacks, the Walkabouts, and Beat Happening. But there were also records by experimental Massachusetts rock band Green Magnet School; indie-rock act Codeine; UK author/musician Billy Childish; and the compilation *The Way of the Vaselines* by the Scottish group the Vaselines, who had broken up in 1989 but were suddenly of interest after Kurt Cobain mentioned how much he liked them in several interviews. The final release of the year was a single by Nick Cave and Shane MacGowan: "What a Wonderful World"/ "Rainy Night in Soho"/ "Lucy."

A *Billboard* story noted the label was focusing on "highly active scenes in other parts of the US and in Canada's Maritime provinces," aided by opening a Sub Pop office in Boston. "We were able to expand and have an East Coast office in Boston, which was run by Joyce Linehan," says Bruce. "Joyce was able to bring in a lot of new artists, such as Sebadoh. This was crucial as most of our Seattle bands had moved on, and we needed some fresh energy. We even had a Sub Pop mini festival in Burlington, Vermont, called 'Vermonstress.'"

"Sub Pop did what all the majors and many indies weren't doing," says Nils. "Bruce and Jon felt confident about their tastes, and about putting out things that were more esoteric. They weren't really thinking about commercial concerns; they were thinking about what they were interested in putting out. The name 'Sub Pop' had clout; bands that a lot of labels wanted to sign would sign to Sub Pop. There was just so much possibility. And it was an awesome time for music in general; it was exciting what the American indie scene had spawned. There were just a lot of great bands, in the early to late '90s, all over the world. Anybody we were into, we had the possibility to have conversations with and to work with, and it was super exciting. And the stuff we were putting out, we were able to support. It felt like everybody was being taken care of, in a way that hadn't always been reliable before."

There was a little expansion in Seattle, too. Sub Pop's first retail store, the Sub Pop Mega Mart—a storefront just under five hundred square feet—opened on October 1, 1993, in the same block as the Terminal Sales Building. The store was set up in part to keep tourists from dropping in at Sub Pop's own offices. "Instead of having people accumulate at the front desk to validate their enthusiasm for grunge and the music of Seattle, we had a little spot around the corner," Rich Jensen explains. "People could go there and take their pictures and hang out and buy some records and not be in the way."

Bruce jokingly described the Mega Mart to the *Seattle Post-Intelligencer* as "a store/archive of Sub Pop paraphernalia for world travelers seeking the holy grail of grunge. People can leave without spending a cent, yet feel a little more enlightened." A press release about the opening noted that the only other retail outlet in the US based around a record label was SST's store in California and added that the first hundred customers to buy a CD at the shop would get a free copy of Nirvana's *Bleach*.

◎ ◎ ◎

"It was just nice to have stability," says Rich. "The main thing was, bills got paid. And the people who had waited a year to get paid—or more—got paid, so that was a good thing." Rich worked hard to get Sub Pop's house in order. Pre-*Nevermind*, the company had never kept on top of things such as studio expenses.

"Prior to that, we didn't even do invoices," says Jack Endino of how Reciprocal had dealt with the company. "We just called them up and said, 'Look, I just had Green River in here and you owe me $600 bucks,' and they would get it in the mail. Once it became less of a fly-by-night amateur operation, I got a call and was told, 'Look, we need to find out what we spent on all these records,' because they started having to account for every nickel and dime. So I basically had to go back through the old log sheets and add it up for them, and say, 'All right, here's what you spent on this band, here's what you spent on that band,' and laid it out for them."

"I tried to bring systems in," Rich explains. "I established a royalty system, I established a production system, helped hire an attorney. And once the company was flush, there were other hirings. We brought in somebody to focus on radio promotion, and really just built a label staff. In terms of controls and so on, I think we could've done a better job. But it's a pretty risky business. And the company's still here, so something must've been done right."

It wasn't all smooth sailing. In July 1993, Sub Pop filed suit against its distributor, Caroline, contending the company had defrauded the label; the suit was settled for an undisclosed sum. "There was a period where there was no distributor," says Rich. "There was just a lot of records in a couple small rooms being mailed out, and we were doing what we could. There was a gap between the relationship with Caroline and the relationship with ADA [the Alternative Distribution Alliance, Sub Pop's next distributor]. ADA hadn't formed yet. So just making it through that period was quite challenging. That's one of the things where I really have to tip my hat to Jonathan, for holding it together during that period of time." ADA was formed with help from Sub Pop; the company owned a 10 percent stake in the business.

There was also a kerfuffle involving one of the label's most notorious bands, punk act the Dwarves (whose members originally came from Chicago but eventually relocated to San Francisco). The Dwarves were committed to being provocative; the cover of their first record for Sub Pop, *Blood, Guts & Pussy* (1990), showed two young women and a small man, all naked and covered in blood (the man covering his genitals with a rabbit), while the back cover listed such titles as "Let's Fuck," "Fuck You Up and Get High," and "Motherfucker." Vocalist Blag Dahlia tried to downplay the outrage. "It wasn't a cheesecake shot, it was an art photo," he said of the cover.

Prior to the release of their 1993 album *Sugarfix*, the band told Sub Pop that their guitarist, HeWhoCannotBeNamed, had been murdered in Philadelphia in April. A press release was duly issued, including information on where to send flowers and condolences. The label then learned that the guitarist was, in fact, alive;

Sub Pop had been pranked by one of its own acts. (It wasn't the first time; when the band felt they weren't being paid promptly enough, they sprayed-painted the words "YOU OWE DWARVES $$" on the floor during a visit to Sub Pop's offices).

Sub Pop was known for its love of hyperbole, but it was felt this stunt crossed a line, and thus required some damage control. "We accepted Blag's defense that it was a 'punk rock' thing to do, in keeping with the spirit of the band," Nils Bernstein wrote in a press release. "The whole ordeal unforgivably overstepped the bounds of media manipulation and self-promotion." The press release concluded by saying that after the release of *Sugarfix*, the Dwarves would be dropped from the label. Dahlia contended the label was in on the joke all along, telling author Greg Prato that Bruce and Jon had loved the idea of spreading the false rumor and had only denied being involved because "they were just frightened and panicked." He also claimed the band hadn't been dropped; *Sugarfix* was the last album they owed Sub Pop on their contract.

For the most part, things were going well for Sub Pop. And yet there was a change, and it was something Bruce felt the most keenly. Bands now came to Sub Pop without any vision of their own, simply wanting to be stars. "They walk into the office—you can spot people like this a mile away—[and] basically say, 'Mold me. I'll do anything you want, just give me an advance,'" he told *Musician*. "Those are exactly the kind of people we shut the door to." To journalist Keith Cameron, he said, "Post-*Nevermind*, the artistic climate really shifted … the vibe got more corporate." Now the talk was about deals, not art, "and I felt a lot of my own personal excitement starting to shift."

It was the first sign of a discontent that would continue to grow. When Megan Jasper first started working for the company, Bruce and Jon took her out for her birthday, and Bruce said to her, "So, have you figured it out yet? I'm the brains, he's the money." The two had often been portrayed that way— Bruce came up with the artistic concepts, Jon handled the finances. "I definitely had the sense that Bruce was more the visionary as far as branding, and brand identity was concerned," says Dan Trager, who was hired in 1993 to handle tour publicity. "But there was no question that Jon was there every day and had more of his feet on the ground as far as an everyday business sort of thing."

Though this was a bit of an oversimplification—Jon had his share of artistic ideas as well—it was rooted in some truth. The two men were different, but in the past their differences had complemented one another. Now they would start to drive them apart.

◉ ◉ ◉

The big news for Sub Pop in early 1994 was Boston's modern lounge act Combustible Edison, whose debut album, *I, Swinger*, led to them being hailed as "the band that poured the first shot in the Cocktail Revolution"—the so-called "Cocktail Nation" movement of the mid-'90s, which saw a revival of interest in the lounge-tiki-exotica music of the '50s and '60s. The group's music would later be picked up for film soundtracks. Sub Pop was quick to profit from this new revenue stream by setting up a licensing department, "which was very proactive," Jon told the *Guardian*. "At the time, independent labels did not have someone doing that, but we did. So the music of Combustible Edison and the music of Pigeonhed generated lots and lots and lots of money and helped sustain the label through some lean times."

The lean times were closer than the company realized. Sub Pop failed to make a profit in 1994, marking the start of a downward slide. But that news was far overshadowed by a sudden tragedy, one that would once again see grunge dominating the headlines: the suicide of Kurt Cobain.

Cobain had never seemed entirely at ease with Nirvana's overwhelming success, and his accelerating heroin use further exacerbated his underlying depression. Following a suicide attempt in Rome on the night of March 3, 1994 (publicly described as an accidental overdose), Cobain had been urged to enter a rehab facility in Los Angeles, which he reluctantly did at the end of the month. But he walked out after two days and returned to Seattle, then dropped out of sight. On April 8, an electrician who arrived to install a security system at Cobain's home discovered his body lying in a room above the property's detached garage.

Seattle rock station KXRX had broken the news at 9:30 a.m., but the initial report only stated that the body of an unidentified white male in his twenties had been found at Cobain's residence. Then Dan Trager received a call from his girlfriend, Courtney Miller, who worked at *The Rocket*. In an odd twist, Miller's former boyfriend, medical student Nikolas Hartshorne, was now working for the King County Medical Examiner's Office; it was Hartshorne who would confirm Cobain's death and perform the autopsy. Courtney called Dan to tell him the news.

Dan was in a daze when he hung up the phone. Just then, Jon walked by his desk, on the way to the conference room. Dan stopped him, saying, "Jon, I hate to be the bearer of bad news, but I can confirm that it was Kurt." Jon's response was one of disbelief: "How can you do that?"

"I told him about the phone call," says Dan. "But he was still hoping I was wrong. Everybody was hoping I was wrong; I was hoping I was wrong. I was hoping that Courtney got it wrong. I was hoping that Nik got it wrong. So there was still an element of like, 'Wait and see,' almost. Denial. Exactly."

"It was pretty awful," says Nils, who knew Kurt was dead as soon as he arrived at Sub Pop and saw the expression on the receptionist's face. "It just was fucked up. People were trying to scale the side of the building, to get up to the terrace at the Terminal Sales Building, and then try to get up to where our office was, which was above that terrace area. Everybody was calling; the receptionist started just picking up phone and saying, 'No comment, no comment.' It was really intense. You couldn't start fielding phone calls, because it would never stop. And so at first, that day, it was just like, 'Fuck. What do we do?' The media aspect of it was a zoo. I had people I didn't know at my apartment, waiting outside, wanting me to give a quote, and a lot of people calling me at home. I was doing press, so journalists had my home phone number as a publicist."

Sub Pop had planned to hold its annual anniversary party on April 9 at the Crocodile Café. At first, there was talk of canceling. But it was ultimately decided that it would be better for the event to go on, and it ended up becoming an unofficial wake for Seattle's music community. "Everybody was just kind of shell-shocked," Nils remembers. "People were crying and everyone was drinking a lot, and it was heavy. Velocity Girl was playing the party, and at one point Sarah [Shannon], the singer, just ran offstage and ran out of the venue. She was crying. It was so heavy and so emotional, I can't imagine being one of the bands trying to play." Pond and Sunny Day Real Estate were also on the bill. "It was just sad and icky," Nils adds.

Another boost of royalties came in due to sales of *Bleach* and other Nirvana releases. It was an unsettling experience. "It was good for business; that's the thing that was really wrenching," says Rich. But then came financial worries of a different kind.

◎ ◎ ◎

Earlier, Sub Pop's problem was that the label didn't have enough money. Now, it almost seemed like having more than enough could be equally problematic.

"I think many of the signings were good, such as Sunny Day Real Estate, Sebadoh, and the Spinanes," says Bruce. "The office culture was becoming more professional, but less spontaneous. Not surprising, considering the size of the new staff. There was a moment when a new hire with a corporate background announced that there would be 'No more brainstorming' at one of our marketing meetings. Interestingly, most of the marketing that Sub Pop became famous for was done prior to this announcement. I would have preferred a more spontaneous culture, with less corporate influence. We were growing into the next Atlantic, when I would have felt more comfortable being the next Rough Trade."

Nonetheless, the idea of forming an alliance with a major label seemed inevitable, says Jon. "Everybody that we came in contact with who was already part of the major label system would keep on advocating, 'You guys have got to do a deal, you're going to lose all your bands,' and blah blah blah. And Bruce and I never really saw it that way because Bruce in particular, to his credit, saw our enterprise as being more of a local familial endeavor as opposed to being a national or even multi-national music company. But we also saw in the wake of a lot of local bands' success that we needed to have additional resources if we wanted to keep playing on the same turf that we were playing on. Not just money, but in terms of money and promotional resources—which I guess is another way of saying money! And so the deals that we contemplated had always been those naïve deals of 'We get to do whatever it is we want to do and hopefully we'll come up with something that you find to be valuable.'"

Back when *Nevermind* was going up the charts, Rich had picked up the phone at Sub Pop one day and found himself talking to financial advisor Dana Giacchetto, who ran a company called the Cassandra Group. "We started a relationship with them that helped us handle our money, when we started to have some," he says. "And that led to conversations in 1993 about trying to structure some kind of a partnership deal to get some more money, to leverage the market position that Bruce and Jon and Sub Pop had achieved. It really knocked people through a loop, throughout the music business, that someone could come from nowhere, from this punk rock weirdo stuff, and knock Michael Jackson and Guns N' Roses off the charts. So we had this idea that we'd be able to sell a minority non-controlling stake in the company to somebody that just wanted to participate in our genius and insight."

Discussions were put on hold after Cobain's death. "Nobody could really think about it," Rich says. But by the fall, they'd resumed. Giacchetto later summarized the offers in a *Hollywood Reporter* profile: Microsoft had put in a bid of $4 million ("paltry … frankly insulting"), Sony Music had bid $5 million, David Geffen had bid $8 million ("I told him his bid was way too f-ing low"), and Universal had been the top bidder at $25 million, "but it wasn't the right creative fit."

Finally, in November 1994, it was announced that Sub Pop was selling a 49 percent interest in the company to Warner Music Group US. The deal would go into effect in 1995. In an official statement, Doug Morris, chairman and CEO of Warner Music US, lauded Sub Pop's achievements as an independent label, while Bruce was quoted as saying, "This partnership will help us achieve our goal of building Sub Pop into a label that combines the vision of an indie with the clout of a major."

"Sub Pop started with a $20 investment," Bruce later told Mark Yarm. "Fifteen years later, the company received a check for $20 million from Time Warner."

"Even now, it just is so crazy," Rich marvels. "Because they paid for a minority stake in the business, so they had no control. Just a year or two before that, 100 percent of Motown was sold for $60 million. So, to be a non-controlling 49 percent of this little operation in Seattle, it was a pretty spectacular transaction." (It was also a rare success for Giacchetto, who would later serve time in prison for fraud; he died in 2016, at the age of fifty-three.)

It all seemed to work out in Sub Pop's favor; the label's founders had retained majority control of the company and could make their own creative decisions. But there would be new obstacles ahead, leading to difficulties that would rival the troubled period of 1991.

"Ironically, we struck an amazing deal with Warner Music Group, but it ended up being an incredible mistake nearly right off the bat," says Jon. "In another ironic twist, it's ended up becoming an amazing relationship. But it took us many years to get there."

# 5
# THE FALLOUT

*Our corporate partners had the expectation we were going to be able to sign another Nirvana. We had a good track record. And so the circumstances came down to Warners having one set of expectations, Bruce having another set, and I having a third set. And that kind of led to a mess.*

—Jon Poneman, "Sub Pop: 25 years of underground rock," the *Guardian*, July 4, 2013

It was a company in crisis. Overextended, not making a profit, yet nonetheless spending money it didn't have. Staffers—those who hadn't been laid off—were upset, threatening revolt. The Supervisory Chairman of Executive Management and the Executive Chairman of Supervisory Management were at odds. There was another local magazine cover (Jon smiling, Bruce looking as if he'd been poked with a sharp stick), with a headline predicting doom: "Sub Popped: Sub Pop's founders try to rescue the legendary record label from 'mutiny,' red ink, and themselves." But it wasn't 1991. It was 1997. History had begun to repeat itself. It all begged the question: Sub Pop—what happened?

The label had entered 1995 with high hopes, now that its founders had the clout of a major label behind them. But seven months after Doug Morris called Sub Pop's achievements as an independent label "the model for the industry," he was fired, a result of the extensive infighting that had emerged in the company in the wake of the death of Warner Communications CEO Steve Ross. At the time, there were six major label companies: BMG, EMI, PolyGram, Sony Music,

Universal Music Group, and the Warner Music Group. By the end of the decade, following mergers between BMG and Sony, and PolyGram and Universal, there would be four.

Power struggles commenced. "As soon as we became partners with [Warner Music Group], everything went to hell," Jon told me in 2005. "There was a certain Shakespearean quality to the whole thing; these people who are stabbing each other in the back, and one person who thinks that they're going to ascend to the chairmanship, and the next thing you know they're out of a job. It was really an incredibly duplicitous environment at the time."

In a later interview, he reflected on the changing terrain at the larger company: "The turnover is so crazy. I have people who have been working here at Sub Pop for more than ten years, and a growing group that worked here for twenty. With Warner alone, I've seen three different ownership teams."

So, Sub Pop's relationship with its new partner hadn't begun on as solid a foundation as had been hoped. But as the label's founders retained majority control of the company, they were still calling all the shots. The influx of major label dollars led to the opening of new offices in Toronto and London. Staff—and salaries—swelled. Sub Pop continued to lose money, but no one was terribly bothered about it—yet.

◎ ◎ ◎

Releases over the next two years offered the same mix of Northwest artists and other acts from around the country and abroad. But in Bruce's view, the label's new money wasn't being handled well. "My observation is that the company would spend money as fast as it came in," he says. "So bringing in more cash resulted in spending more like a major label. Of course, the majors were being very aggressive in trying to sign any artist we were looking at, so it was a challenging situation."

He points to Sub Pop's signing of Memphis band the Grifters as an example. When one of the label's A&R reps told him the band could be signed for $5,000, he was agreeable. He was astonished when he later learned that the band ended up being signed for $150,000. Their first album, *Ain't My Lookout*, sold a mere five thousand copies.

"We found ourselves going from being the little rascals playing in the music industry to suddenly competing for bands in our own social group who were being lured by Sony Music or BMG, even our own business partners at Warner," Jon observed to the *Guardian*.

"I had a lot to learn about the music industry," he admits. "When we did this deal with Warner, we had the idea that we would somehow be the label that we had been, but we would also have the resources of a major label. Now, in retrospect, I realize that I had no fucking clue what I was talking about."

The label was increasingly seen to be losing its identity. A *Seattle Times* feature, "Beyond Grunge at Sub Pop," portrayed the label's best days as being behind it: "Sub Pop may have more capital, but as a shaper of tastes, its most rarified days have probably passed."

There was a sense that the label was boxing outside its weight. "Trying to go head-to-head, [to] appear like we had the intimacy of an indie but the muscle of a major label, and we ended up having neither," Jon told *Pitchfork*. To this writer, he also admitted that he felt Sub Pop was losing its way at the time: "I championed some records that I think in retrospect were inappropriate for the label. I also think that our bad business practices caught up with us and distracted us from what our mission really was, which was to put out great music, and have meaningful and successful relationships with our artists. I was asleep at the wheel for a few years there."

"There was tension as to what direction the label should be taking," says Dan Trager. "It was like the 'White Album' years of the Beatles, in terms of,

'Well, we should be doing this.' 'No, we should be doing this.' 'Well, we should do it all.' 'Well, no, we can't afford to do it all.' A lot of going around in circles, chasing tails, and pointing fingers was going on."

A persistent problem was that releases that were expected to sell were underperforming. *Diary* (1994), the debut album by the dreamy, emo Seattle band Sunny Day Real Estate, was both a critical and commercial success, eventually selling nearly a quarter of a million copies. But inner tensions split the band before they'd even completed their second album, with lead singer Jeremy Enigk attributing the split jointly to his spiritual awakening and his fears of a "rock star life." Without a working band to promote *LP2*, which was released in 1995, sales sagged. Nor did records like the Supersuckers' *The Sacrilicious Sounds of the Supersuckers* (1995), Jeremy Enigk's solo debut *Return of the Frog Queen* (1996), and Sebadoh's *Harmacy* (1996) sell as well as had been hoped. According to Sebadoh lead singer and guitarist Lou Barlow, Sub Pop spent a lot of money on radio promotion and trying to place the band's song "Willing to Wait" on *Friends* but to no avail.

As Nils Bernstein recalls, "There became a real focus on commercial radio, which felt appropriate for only some of the bands, and maybe a lopsided distribution of our resources. And so there was some frustration around that. Sub Pop was really trying to be like, well, maybe if we put huge investments in these places—and this is something that was happening before Warner—it'll pay off for some artist. Eric Matthews, Sebadoh; one of these artists will be really huge, and it'll justify these expenses. So they're opening offices around the world. They're hiring independent promoters and consultants, and they're doing this level of investment which is kind of dangerous."

"Part of the identity crisis was following up the success of Nirvana, and trying to metamorphose into this competitive major label scenario," says Dan. "Well, if you sell two thousand records, in one sense that's pretty good. But in the sense of comparing yourself to the mainstream market, it's nothing; every record was a failure."

Musically, Sub Pop seemed to have no clear aesthetic; stylistically, its releases were all over the map. There were records by Detroit blues singer Thornetta Davis (*Sunday Morning Music*, 1996), instrumental lounge-rock act Friends of Dean Martinez (*The Shadow of Your Smile*, 1995), Chicago funk band 5ive Style (*5ive Style*, 1995), and even the Beach Boys, who released a single containing previously unreleased tracks from their legendary *Pet Sounds* sessions in 1996 (a stereo mix of "I Just Wasn't Made for These Times," a vocals-only mix of "Wouldn't It Be Nice," and the backing track of "Here Today"). It was a roster that *The Rocket* called "artistically ambitious, but almost to a fault."

Nineteen ninety-six was also the year grunge became nostalgia, as the focus of Doug Pray's documentary about the Seattle music scene, *Hype!* Sub Pop would release the film's soundtrack on CD; there was also a limited-edition box of four singles on colored vinyl.

Given Bruce and Jon's chummy camaraderie in *Hype!*, it was ironic that by the time of the film's release in November 1996, Bruce had left Sub Pop, officially resigning from the company in April of that year. He'd been gradually dropping out of working day-to-day at the label following the birth of his first child. "The day after my daughter Iris was born—August 28, 1993—I started telecommuting so that I could spend time with her," he explains. "That was a very conscious decision that had nothing to do with what was going on with the label. In addition to working from my home, I came to the office every week for meetings. I was still very active with Sub Pop; I just answered my e-mails from home."

But over the years, he'd become disenchanted—especially as he felt that a company that had started out mocking corporate culture had started emulating that very culture too much for his tastes. "'Indie' culture was starting to become less and less interesting to me," he says. "Post-*Nevermind*, there seemed to be less art students and more business majors starting bands. Artists talked more about deals, less about art or politics. I had been in the indie trenches with Sub Pop since 1980. Sub Pop went from writing about the Dead Kennedys to convincing pro basketball players to wear our T-shirts. Snooze."

Speaking about his partner's departure nearly ten years later, Jon said he understood Bruce's reasons for leaving. "Bruce founded this company and really set the agenda in a lot of ways," he says. "He certainly established the aesthetic for the company, and was really instrumental in getting things off the ground. Having said that, he split pretty early. His priorities changed. And I think particularly Nirvana's leaving and going on to Geffen was very demoralizing for him. Not so much from the business standpoint but just the feeling that anybody and anything could be bought and sold in the marketplace. And he thought that our relationship was grounded more on common values, and not so much on dollars and cents. That did indeed set the stage for his eventually leaving Sub Pop.

"The other thing is, Bruce really liked Sub Pop being small and a little bit more—he liked a higher degree of, as he put it, *spontaneity* in the company. Which I could appreciate. But there was also a certain amount of anarchy in the company. Which in the music industry, given that neither of us were business people, spontaneity was synonymous with anarchy."

But however much Jon had adapted to Sub Pop's becoming a more structured business environment, and however much he'd enjoyed the label's sudden flush of success, the dramatic changes the company had gone through since 1991 were also stressful for him. He was tired.

"After we did the deal with Warner, I was so burned out," he says. "I longed for some meaningful mentoring. Getting into business with Warner, and doing the kind of business that we were doing with our artists, with their expectations, which were colored by the times—all of us had crazy expectations.

Jonathan Poneman and Bruce Pavitt on the roof of the Terminal
Sales Building, home of the Sub Pop offices, 1990.

*Subterranean Pop* issue #2, November 1980. Bruce asked fellow
Evergreen student Lynda Barry to provide the cover art.

*Sub Pop 200* compilation, December 1988, featuring TAD, the Fluid, Nirvana, Mudhoney, Soundgarden, Green River, Fastbacks, Screaming Trees, and others. Cover art by another Evergreen student, Charles Burns.

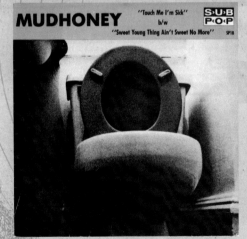
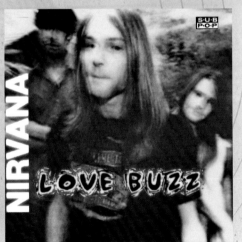

**A sampling of Sub Pop releases from the late 1980s:**
Soundgarden's debut single, "Hunted Down" / Green River – *Dry as a Bone* EP
Mudhoney – "Touch Me I'm Sick" single / Nirvana's debut single, "Love Buzz"

SONIC YOUTH
"Touch Me I'm Sick"
EDITION OF 3000
Photo by Charles Peterson. Recorded by Wharton Tiers at Wharton Tiers Studio, NYC.

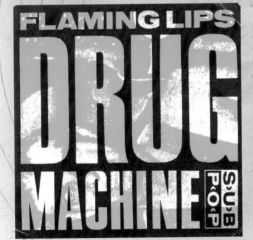

FLAMING LIPS
DRUG MACHINE
S·U·B P·O·P

AFGHAN WHIGS
I Am The Sticks b/w White Trash Party
S·U·B P·O·P
SP32
Recorded January 1989 at Kit City, Indianapolis. Produced by Paul Mahern & Greg Dulli. Engineered by Paul Mahern, second engineer Lee Cuthbert.

**A further sampling of Sub Pop releases from the late 1980s:**
Sonic Youth – "Halloween" single / TAD's debut album, *God's Balls*
Flaming Lips' debut single, "Drug Machine" / Afghan Whigs' debut single, "I Am the Sticks"

Jack Endino, who produced virtually all the early Sub Pop releases, at Reciprocal Studio, 2002.

Daniel House, the Skin Yard bassist who became Sub Pop's Director of Sales and Distribution, at his desk in 1988.

Kurt Cobain with Nils Bernstein, the owner of the Rebellious Jukebox record store who was hired to handle retail promotion for Sub Pop. Western Washington University, Bellingham, 1992.

Nirvana performing for a Sub Pop showcase at the Center on Contemporary Art in Seattle, August 1989. Note Kurt Cobain's Sub Pop 200 t-shirt.

Nils Bernstein's Rebellious Jukebox record store, 1991.

Bruce backstage at Pearl Jam's Drop in the Park, Magnuson Park, 1992.

Jonathan Poneman at the Spar Cafe, Olympia, early '90s. Note Krist Novoselic in the background.

## Lexicon of Grunge: Breaking the Code

All subcultures speak in code; grunge is no exception. Megan Jasper, a 25-year-old sales representative at Caroline Records in Seattle, provided this lexicon of grunge-speak, coming soon to a high school or mall near you:

**WACK SLACKS:** Old ripped jeans

**FUZZ:** Heavy wool sweaters

**PLATS:** Platform shoes

**KICKERS:** Heavy boots

**SWINGIN' ON THE FLIPPITY-FLOP:** Hanging out

**BOUND AND HAGGED:** Staying home on Friday or Saturday night

**SCORE:** Great

**HARSH REALM:** Bummer

**COB NOBBLER:** Loser

**DISH:** Desirable guy

**BLOATED, BIG BAG OF BLOATATION:** Drunk

**LAMESTAIN:** Uncool person

**TOM-TOM CLUB:** Uncool outsiders

**ROCK ON:** A happy goodbye

(L) The infamous Lexicon of Grunge that Megan Jasper created as a joke for a *New York Times* reporter who took her all too seriously. (R) Megan Jasper at the Crocodile Café, ca. 1992.

Top photo: Intern Laura Wetherholt, Jonathan, and Bruce in the Sub Pop offices, ca. 1992. Bottom photo: Tad Doyle and Kurt Danielson of the band TAD backstage at a Mudhoney show, Motorsports International Garage, 1990.

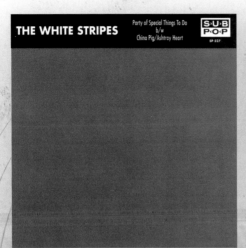

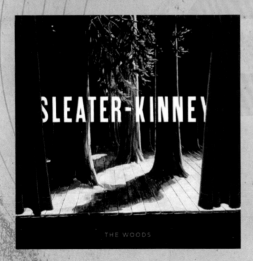

**A sampling of Sub Pop releases from the new millennium:**
The White Stripes' "Party of Special Things to Do" single / The Postal Service's "Such Great
Heights" single / Sleater-Kinney's *The Woods* album / The Shins' *Wincing the Night Away* album

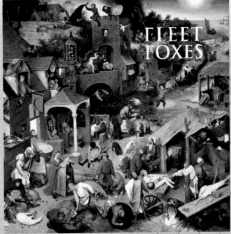

**A further sampling of Sub Pop releases from the new millennium:**
Flight of the Conchords' self-titled album / Fleet Foxes' self-titled album
The Head and the Heart's self-titled album / Father John Misty's *I Love You, Honeybear* album

Beach House (top) and Band of Horses (bottom) made their respective Sub Pop debuts in 2006,

Shabazz Palaces, one of the few hip hop acts signed to Sub Pop.
They released their debut album for the label in 2011.

Bruce Pavitt and Jonathan Poneman in May 2018, thirty years after founding Sub Pop Records.

And I just got burned out. I didn't even realize to what degree I was just on remote control. But that had a lot of effect on the company. That also as well from a management standpoint, I really—I felt like I was absentee."

There were also underlying complications because of how the original deal with Warner had been arranged. "Usually, when you do a deal like this, it's company-to-company," Jon explains. "But we did a deal where it was individuals to Warner. So Bruce and I got paid the money, and then kicked money back into Sub Pop for operations. And Bruce put in his money with the understanding that if we ran a tight ship we should be a pretty financially stable organization and he should be able to get dividends and all should be fine.

"But our bills had gotten out of control. We signed a bunch of things that didn't pan out. We were spending too much money. I was continuing to pump money into the company, but it was ultimately unsustainable. Bruce was grousing about not getting any money out of the company, and wondering why this was happening. And the reason why was because I was spending all this money—my money—to keep it afloat.

"I figured that Bruce and I were heading for a calamity. But I believed that I would either be able to talk him down out of the situation, or else it was something I could kick down the road a bit. But there was a real philosophical difference. And I can understand better now than I could then why Bruce felt the way that he did. By any way that you measure it, the company was mismanaged at that time. It's not to say that there weren't pockets of good management, good intention, and there was plenty of talent and talented artists. But the enterprise, taken holistically, was not being run in a sustainable way."

◎ ◎ ◎

All of this set the stage for what became known in the company's history as "the coup."

As 1997 began, there was an underlying malaise at the label. "The fact of the matter was, Sub Pop was not a very nice place to work at that point," Jon said. The previous months had seen 20 percent of the staff fired or laid off, according to one staffer. Jon and Bruce (who, despite having resigned, still held a 25 percent stake in the company) had set up a meeting with Warner Music Group in February to discuss business matters.

Meanwhile, some of the staff, including Nils Bernstein, began discussing the situation amongst themselves, and met with Bruce at Linda's Tavern (a bar Bruce and Jon had invested in). "I felt like Bruce was really frustrated for a long time," says Nils. "At the time, I was very aligned with Bruce's point of view about things, and frustrated with Jonathan's point of view. What Bruce was saying and doing made more sense to me, so I was more supportive of that. In retrospect, I can see where that was maybe just idealism. Everything fell to Jonathan, and he had to figure out a way to maintain this growing company and manage all these people and offices, while not just without the support of Bruce, but with some antagonism from Bruce. And in retrospect I can see where that's really difficult and unfair to Jonathan. But at the time I was like, Bruce is right. It just felt like the whole thing that Sub Pop and our whole scene was against, the corporate ogre, we'd become, and we needed to get back to our credible roots. Who's Team Bruce? Let's save Sub Pop!"

"A lot of very unhappy people came to me, and I said 'Let's make your voice heard,'" Bruce later told the *Seattle Weekly*. "My basic feeling is that I agreed with most of what they were saying, and I tried to persuade people in the organization that these people had some good points." But when Bruce reached out to Jon, he was met with resistance. Staffers told the *Seattle Weekly* that Bruce and Jon each threatened to sell their shares if the other didn't leave.

Nils was among a group of staffers who decided to make their own case, writing a letter they intended to present to Warner. The letter expressed concern about the "bloat that had come to characterize the label … the amount of money we were spending on records, and by extension on staff, on independent contractors, on offices outside of Seattle," says Nils. "It was about not wanting to get into the major label trap of having one or two bands that float all the other bands. We felt like we could go to being a very profitable company where every record is selling its goal, rather than having to set unrealistic goals because of the amount of money that we were spending on certain things. And it had to do with certain employees, and who should be doing what, and who was effective and who wasn't. It was very cocky.

"We really felt like we were helping," he continues. "We thought, okay, for whatever reason, Bruce and Jon don't feel that they can make these changes. But maybe Warner can force the changes that they're not able to make; all we need is for Warner to sign off on all these changes that Bruce and Jon really want made. So we're kind of helping them by taking the heat off them. And then we'll save the day, and Sub Pop will get back to where everybody wants it to be."

Not everyone who worked at Sub Pop knew about the letter, but even the staffers who weren't involved knew something was up. "It was sort of like *Fight Club*, if you will," Dan says. "There was something going on, and those that were involved were sort of furtively getting together and running to one another's desks. And if you walked in their room, it was one of those weird awkward moments where obviously there was something going on, but we're going to pretend that it wasn't. 'What's going on?' 'Oh, we're just working on trying not to look like we're working on something that we don't want you to know that we're working on.'"

Those who did know more of what was going on were dismayed. According to Rich, who had by then become the label's sub-president, "It was like being the child of a divorce; your parents are fighting. For me, personally, it was difficult, because when I heard that Bruce wanted to come back and play more of an active role in the company, my initial reaction was 'Great!' I was delighted to hear that he wanted to come back. Then he let me know that part of what he was hoping to do was to put other people in charge, and he didn't want me to have a role in the company at that time. I got this by an email from him. So my email back to him was, 'Well, my problem is that Jonathan wants me to stay, and you want me to go, so you guys figure it out.'"

Jon had been distracted by a personal crisis: his father's illness and imminent death. But he knew something was afoot, having, as he puts it, "browbeat" his personal assistant, Keith Rinick, to learn the details. When he finally read the letter, he found he agreed with much of what it said.

"All the things that they suggested that we needed to do, we ultimately did," he says. "And even at the time I thought that it was sound advice. There were a few things, like making certain people president of the company, title changes and stuff like that, that I didn't think really spoke to the issues at hand. But the idea of closing offices that we really didn't need was incredibly obvious."

But Jon also didn't want news of a potential staff revolt to color the upcoming meeting with Warner. While the *Seattle Weekly* said the meeting was so Sub Pop could "beg for more cash" from Warner, Rich Jensen says otherwise. "We were in a dispute at the time with Warner Music about the partnership," he explains, "and we felt that they owed us a certain amount of money. I think that some people in the company thought that there was a begging situation going on, when in fact it was an argument with the partner that 'You owe this.' And so there was some misunderstanding about what was going on; there were a lot of motivations in conflict, and people didn't necessarily have all the information.

"What I knew was, there was a pretty big staff, forty people, who expected to be able to pay for their rent and their groceries and their medical care. And that was at jeopardy; if our partner didn't follow through on their obligation, it would cause a crisis for the label and for the staff. So my allegiance was to the staff, and to see through this conversation we were having with the partner."

In Rich's view, the staff's demands "put Jonathan in a kind of 'take it or leave it' situation, and he didn't want to do that. It just was handled really poorly. It was a challenge to his vision and to the situation in the company at the time."

"The thing that I was afraid of doing was demonstrating any instability to Warner," says Jon. "Because Warner I had always sensed was ready to find an excuse to come in and shut us down. It was like this weird kabuki dance. It's like on one hand we were trying to be autonomous, but on the other hand we were trying to garner their favor at the same time."

So, feeling his authority had been undermined, on Sunday, February 23, Jon fired the four people who had signed the letter: Nils, Keith, artist-support rep Diane Perini, and production coordinator Stacy Shelley. He informed them by telephone. Later, in an interview with online music site *Addicted to Noise*, Jon said that the employees' concerns "were very valid," but added that "when they are put forward in such a manner that they are potentially threatening to my position, I have no choice to act and get that threat out of my way."

"In retrospect, what we were doing was choosing sides in a Bruce/Jon battle and letting Warner Bros. be the arbiters," Nils says today. "I think we all stand by what we wrote. It was just stupid to write it, stupid the way we went about it."

A press release was issued on February 24, attributing the firings to "philosophical differences with the label … The decision was extremely difficult but ultimately in the best interest of the company and associated artists." This angered Bruce, who sent out his own statement, which was printed in the March

20 issue of *The Stranger* (a Seattle weekly). After thanking the four employees "for their years of hard work at Sub Pop," he continued:

> Although current management has every right to shape the company to their satisfaction, I personally feel the departure of these individuals is a tremendous loss for the record label … considering that these individuals were immediately let go after composing a letter outlining grievances, one has to question the motives for dismissal. Were these people canned for expressing their opinions? If so, what does that say about the values and culture of the company?
>
> Bruce Pavitt
> Founder, Co-Chairman, Sub Pop.

The meeting with Warner went ahead on February 25. Two weeks later, Warner Music executive Aaron Levy came to Seattle to get a closer look at how Sub Pop operated. He later publicly stated, "We look forward to continuing what has been a very productive relationship." The crisis had been averted but not without cost. Some of the staff members who hadn't been involved in the coup attempt were left discomfited, unsure of what had just happened.

Dan Trager recalls a staff meeting held in the wake of the firings as "super-duper awkward … there was sort of the question, who's going to stay, who's going to leave, whose side are you on, lines are being drawn. And I'm like, oh, this is not something that resonates with me. This is something that makes me feel deeply uncomfortable, this is not why I'm here. Looking back on it, it was more than anything a reflection of a baby organization having growing pains."

"If I had it to do all over again, I would've done something much different," Jon says today. "The first thing I would've done is spoken to Bruce, and I would've spoken to him more directly. And I would've had frank conversations with people earlier on. I would've created a situation where that letter wouldn't have had to be written. The thing about that is, for that to have happened, I would've had to have been less fried than I was.

"At every juncture, there are things that would've been different. And that's not to say that I'm beyond making mistakes now—I make them all the time. But those were really rookie errors. For me it was a combination of burnout and lack of mentorship. I got into a mentality where I was just trying [to] get through this to the other side. Which was, there was no other side. It was just enduring these bad times in the hope that—it's kind of like getting a hit record. You set everything up, you hope the people like it, but you ultimately need to have some luck for it to be able to work out. And I was kind of relying on the same voodoo to save the company."

Bruce and Jon's relationship was fractured by the coup attempt as well. There was talk of Bruce setting up a subsidiary label within Sub Pop, focused on electronic music, but it came to nothing. While Jon says the two remained civil with each other, according to Bruce, they didn't speak, except through their attorneys, for the next six years.

◎ ◎ ◎

Downsizing continued. The Boston, Toronto, and London offices were all closed. In November 1997, five more employees were let go, in an attempt to "increase efficiency, reduce redundancy, and prepare for a general restructuring of Sub Pop's sales, marketing, and promotion efforts," according to a press release. "With these changes Sub Pop looks forward to being able to better serve the needs of our artists and promote their records more effectively."

It was also announced that there were two new hires, including Megan Jasper. After working for Caroline, Megan had moved on to ADA. As a longtime friend of Jon's, she was aware of the turmoil at the Sub Pop, and her friends had advised her to not return to the company. "I knew it was a risky move," she says. "But Sub Pop's potential was never lost on me. And it seemed like it was in need of something so desperately. I didn't know what that something was. But to have a hand at bringing it back to a place that felt positive and healthy was very attractive to me."

She came back to a company where "the morale was down like I'd never seen it. The employees refused to wear Sub Pop shirts or sweatshirts. They were embarrassed by it."

In an effort to bring people together, Megan set up staff meetings on Tuesday and Thursday mornings. "And I brought in bagels," she says. "I figured if people didn't want to come in and sit, they'd at least want a bagel. So I lured people in. We still do Tuesday and Thursday morning meetings to this day. Because I felt like maybe if we open up communication and people feel like they know what's happening, maybe that will make things a little bit better. Especially after losing so many co-workers."

Though hired as a senior product manager, Megan found herself working with other departments as well. "Other people in the company were coming up to me, saying, 'Hey, I need some of your time, too,'" she says. "And I thought, 'You know what? I'm just going to check in with a lot of people and find out who needs what, and see if I can have a hand at trying to make that better.' I can have a little border collie in me; I like to corral people. And I like working as a team. I can work by myself. But I like people, I like being around people, I like getting everyone together and moving forward together. And I think Jon was hungry for that kind of energy. I could see things with fresh eyes compared to people who had been there for a bit."

She also worked to solicit Jon's involvement. "There was a moment in 1998 when I had to start working on budgets and projections for the following year," she recalls. "The system that we had, I'd been there long enough to where

I knew the way that they were doing it—it was just fucked up, to be honest. There's no pretty way to put it. And that didn't work for me. And so I just thought, 'I'm gonna fuckin' take a crack at this.' And I tried, but I was also feeling stumped with some of my numbers. And so I said to J.P., 'Hey, would you have any interest in working with me and trying to develop this? I want to see if we can make something real that we can actually use throughout the year. And I want to base marketing budgets off of it.' And he sat down, and if I remember, we spent two days together really knocking this thing out. And in my mind, that was a turning point. Because he engaged in a deeper way that I hadn't seen him do in a long time."

Publicly, Sub Pop was still seen to be struggling. *Rolling Stone*'s November 12, 1998, issue included a short article (entitled—what else?—"Sub Popped?") that stated, "The party may finally be over for Sub Pop ... its future looks bleak." It was noted that expected big sellers still failed to perform. The Jesus and Mary Chain's *Munki*, for which sales of one hundred and fifty thousand had been projected, sold fifteen thousand copies. And sales for Sunny Day Real Estate's reunion album, *How It Feels to Be Something On*, stalled at sixty-nine thousand. It was even speculated that Warner Music Group would end up buying out Sub Pop, with an anonymous source quoted as saying, "Warner will come in and pick up the pieces at a greatly reduced rate. It will be the garage sale of the century."

But for Jon, the future didn't look bleak at all. "I got off autopilot," he says. A key signing of the period was Seattle's Murder City Devils. The band had formed in 1996 and released two singles before coming to Sub Pop's attention. They were initially signed to Die Young Stay Pretty, a subsidiary label Sub Pop had set up to issue one-off releases as a quicker, cheaper way of getting a record out. The band's self-titled debut album was released in 1997 and sold four thousand copies—enough to land them a contract with Sub Pop proper.

The band's second album, *Empty Bottles, Broken Hearts*, released in 1998, solidified their popularity. Kathleen Wilson, one of the group's biggest local supporters, wrote in the *Stranger*, "Whether you thought of the Murder City Devils as a group whose powerhouse albums and ebullient live shows were driven by a love of their music and audience, or considered them to be overhyped hipsters who didn't deserve the attention the *Stranger* lavished on them, no one can deny they've left a mark on the Seattle rock scene as indelible as the skull-and-crossbones tattoos that signify their image."

"I think our relationship with the Murder City Devils helped out a lot because it was a local band who would come into the office regularly," says Jon. "And it was a kind of music that was much more familiar to us, and that people expected from Sub Pop originally." He viewed the band as part of a "rock 'n' roll signing spree" the label was pursuing, which included Detroit's The Go, whose debut album, 1999's *Whatcha Doin'*, featured a pre–White Stripes Jack White on lead guitar; the Black Halos, from Vancouver, BC, who were also initially signed to Die Young Stay Pretty; Gardener, featuring Van Conner from Screaming Trees and Aaron Stauffer from Seaweed; and Zen Guerrilla, from San Francisco. They also reached overseas, releasing the second and third albums by Swedish hard-rock band the Hellacopters.

"That was basically the whole zeitgeist of Seattle at that time, that late '90s, early 2000s rock revival," says Jack Endino, who produced the Murder City Devils, the Black Halos, and Zen Guerilla. "I'd spent most of the '90s away from Seattle, because of the big hangover that was happening here. There just weren't any good bands. Nobody wanted to rock, everybody was obsessed with Elastica and Fred Durst; there was just a lot of bad nu-metal and a lot of terrible grunge clones. Then there was a specific thing that came about in '98, which was that the grunge hangover was over with, and people weren't really doing grunge anymore but it was okay to rock again. It culminated in me doing the Hot Hot

Heat record [2002's *Make Up the Breakdown*]; that was one of the last big records I did for Sub Pop in that particular wave of records. That album, at that time, was Sub Pop's biggest record since *Bleach*."

There was also new life for the Sub Pop Singles Club, which was revived to celebrate the label's tenth anniversary. The first release was the Jesus and Mary Chain's "Birthday"/ "Hide Myself," released in April in a limited-edition run of two thousand copies on clear blue vinyl. Subsequent releases included records by Bonnie "Prince" Billy, the White Stripes, Beachwood Sparks, J. Mascis, and Modest Mouse.

And despite the fact that Sub Pop had lost money for four straight years, Jon felt confident about the future. In 1999, in a *Rocket* cover story, he said, "I am re-inaugurating the ages of Northwest rock 'n' roll. That's by and large what we've always been and what we will continue to be as long as there is Sub Pop." (*The Rocket* cover artwork featured a great parody of Charles Burns's *Sub Pop 200* cover art; in the Pat Moriarity/Jim Blanchard illustration, the monkey tied to the guitarist's back in Burns's piece has become a business suit-attired executive, studying a profit-and-loss statement.)

"I think Sub Pop is in the best shape that it's ever been in," he said in the same article. "The mythical good ol' days weren't that great at all. This is our golden age, to be honest. But it's taken a lot of work and a lot of lessons getting there."

# 6

# REBIRTH

*SUB POP 1988–2003: 10 YEARS OF GREAT RECORDS*

—Invitation to Sub Pop's anniversary party, April 27, 2003

On January 19, 2000, Sub Pop released its five-hundredth record, Mudhoney's *March to Fuzz*. The band were not actually on the label at the time (they'd signed to Reprise in 1992), but it was nonetheless fitting that Sub Pop's flagship band would be on SP500. The two-CD set had highlights from the group's grunge heyday ("Suck You Dry," "In 'n' Out of Grace," "Sweet Young Thing Ain't Sweet No More," and, of course, "Touch Me I'm Sick"), along with a second disc of rarities, including such perhaps unlikely covers as Elvis Costello's "Pump It Up," Jimmie Dale Gilmore's "Holden," and Roxy Music's "Editions of You."

It was a release that harkened back to another era. And, as Sub Pop stood on the brink of the twenty-first century, a different era was coming to an end as well. When the lease ran out on Sub Pop's World Domination HQ in the Terminal Sales Building in 1999, it was not renewed. The building's management had sent a letter to the company advising a move. "I remember the letter," says Sub Pop publicist Steve Manning. "'Your business may be better suited to another type of building.'" The wild assortment of musicians coming and going likely raised eyebrows. "It did sort of feel like we were sort of the ugly stepchild," Steve says.

The company ended up moving a few blocks north, to 2514 Fourth Avenue, in Seattle's Belltown neighborhood. At the time of the move, Sub Pop had offices on three floors at the Terminal Sales Building; now they were in a smaller space, "all kind of on top of each other," Steve recalls. "At first it just seemed like, 'Nah, now we've gotta be in this space?' 'We've gotta share a bathroom with the coffee shop next door?' Oh my God, that was horrible. It felt like a sandwich shop; people would come in and ask if they could get a sandwich. It looked like 'Sub Pop' said 'Sub Shop.'"

Tony Kiewel, who was then doing radio promotion for the label (he later moved on to A&R), recalled that one time a vagrant walked into the offices, made a beeline for the kitchen area, poured a packet of Emergenc-C vitamin powder into a bowl, and filled it with hot water. "He started eating it like it was soup," says Tony. "He walked in like he knew the place. We had to say, 'Sir? We're going to have to ask you to leave.'"

But the move also had the unintended effect of bringing the staff closer together. "It was totally a good thing," says Jon. "I think that it had a lot to do with our being able to reconnect with each other, all being on the same floor in the same office."

"It was really good for the way we worked," Steve agrees. "We could fire ideas off each other all day long. That doesn't really happen when you're on three floors." In the old building, Steve, who worked on another floor, might not see Jon for days. Now the staff saw the company president every day. "I felt a much stronger sense of leadership from Jon when we moved into the new building," says Steve. "I think the move reengaged him to some degree. And I also think that he is so well balanced out by Megan, and she was definitely coming into her own in that role at that same time."

Tony Kiewel had arrived at the company in July 2000, moving from Los Angeles, where he'd been working for DreamWorks Records. At the time, some of the late-'90s malaise still hung over the label. "People were telling me not to move here, like, 'You're crazy!'" he says. "It didn't feel like it was necessarily a 100 percent good idea to put a Sub Pop sticker on your car at the time. And it was financially a tough time for Sub Pop. We were all trying to make it work. And Jonathan was doubling down on the company. It felt like, 'Why wouldn't you just walk away? This is not working right now.'"

But Sub Pop was on the verge of another breakthrough. Local band Modest Mouse (who'd released singles on Sub Pop, but primarily recorded for another local label, Up Records, before moving on to Epic Records) had toured with a band from Albuquerque, New Mexico, called the Shins. The group was then a side project for singer/guitarist James Mercer, whose primary band was called Flake Music. So when Isaac Brock, Modest Mouse's lead singer and guitarist, gave Dan Trager a Flake Music recording, he assured him, "They're better than this now, but here's what the old band sounds like."

Even music by "the old band" was enough to convince Jon. "I said, 'Oh my God, this is amazing, you've got to get a hold of them,'" he recalls. Dan managed to track down a manager, "but I just was not getting a hold of the band."

Flake Music broke up in 1999, by which time the Shins had begun releasing their own recordings. Jon next heard of the group when Zeke Howard, drummer for Love as Laughter, an Olympia band who'd signed with Sub Pop in 1999, brought back CDs of the Shins' music he'd picked up while on tour. "And, according to Zeke, he said he gave one CD to [Up Records co-founder] Chris Takino, and Chris allegedly said that it sounded too much like Built to Spill," says Jon. "But he gave the other CD to me, and I was like, 'Oh my God, this is the greatest thing in the world!' And then I sent Shawn [Rogers] and Stewart [Meyer] from my office down to Albuquerque to watch them play, and hang out with them. That's what happened."

Despite his excitement, Jon admitted to being "gun-shy" about signing the band. "I had championed so many records that I thought were great, but were wholly misunderstood by the grunge-loving, late-'90s Sub Pop audience," he explained to the *Guardian*, and certainly the band's dreamy pop wasn't the kind of music people usually associated with Sub Pop. The label initially only offered to put out one single, but after listening to the band's latest music, the contract was upgraded to a three-album deal. The single "New Slang" was released in February 2001, with the album *Oh, Inverted World* following in June.

"That was the band that, hands down, everyone in the company agreed this was something special—this was something where we need to go all in right now," says Megan Jasper. "I remember Chris Jacobs, our publicist then, saying, 'It was the first time I ever just sent music to writers and said—I'm not even going to sell this, just listen to it. I was so confident with how it would be met.' And he was right."

Nonetheless, initial expectations for the album were modest; it was hoped sales might reach ten thousand. But the band began attracting more attention when "New Slang" was used in a McDonald's commercial in 2002, something Steve Manning credits as helping to change the perception of rock bands licensing their music. "At the time, it created a ton of negative feedback: 'Sell outs!' 'What are you doing?'" he says. "It became a conversation in the music industry online: 'Is that cool?' or 'Can you do that?' Which I think now, here we are ten years later, and it's become the most common way for artists to make money. Independent artists can get their songs on TV shows or in commercials and actually get paid. So yeah, it's really interesting to see the industry now."

In 2017, James Mercer told Australian website *TheMusic* that he regretted allowing the band's music to be used in the commercial, because it alienated some of their fans. But many more had been drawn in: a year after the album's release, it had sold ninety thousand copies. A further boost came when "New Slang" was featured in the 2004 film *Garden State*; Natalie Portman's character insists that the film's lead character (played by Zach Braff, also the film's screenwriter and director) listen to the song, saying, "You gotta hear this one song—it'll change your life, I swear." The film's soundtrack (on Epic Records), also featured the Shins' "Caring Is Creepy," and would win a Grammy for "Best Compilation Soundtrack Album for Motion Pictures, Television, or Other Visual Media."

*Oh, Inverted World* would eventually sell over half a million copies. The album's success "locked us in as a team," says Megan. "It allowed us to grow some muscle, and to learn new things about how to market a record, and working with an artist. That band taught us a lot. They taught us how to operate really well as a group. They taught us strategies, because we hadn't worked with bands that were growing that quickly. So we had to sit and really talk through marketing strategies, retail strategies. They taught us to think outside the box. We knew that this was a band where the people who loved their music felt this ownership with them. And so how do you keep that sense of ownership with this band that's growing very quickly; how do we keep that feeling like a secret, even when it's not a secret? So we had to really talk through new ways of marketing. And it made us better in so many ways."

◎ ◎ ◎

The band's success breathed new life into Sub Pop. "It had every bit the impact on the label this century that Nirvana did in the last," Jon told the *Guardian*. "It empowered all of the bands from a commercial perspective."

Further commercial success arrived in 2003, with the release of *Give Up* by the Postal Service. The group had started as a side project for Ben Gibbard of Death Cab for Cutie (founded in Bellingham, Washington), and Los Angeles–based electronic artist/DJ Jimmy Tamborello (aka Dntel). The two first worked together when Ben contributed vocals to "(This Is) the Dream of Evan and Chan," a track on Dntel's 2001 album *Life Is Full of Possibilities*. After completing work on the track, Jimmy was up in Seattle, visiting Ben and Tony Kiewel, who had been roommates with Jimmy in LA.

"We were just talking about how great that song was," Tony recalls. "And they were talking about how much fun it was to do that song, and 'Maybe we should do another one!' They were like, 'Maybe we'll do a whole EP.'

"And then I was like, 'Maybe you should do a whole album. Because if you're going to do an EP, you might as well do an album. I bet Sub Pop would do it if you did one.'

"'You think so? That might be kind of fun. Let's do that.' It was like, get drunk, hang out, 'Yeah, let's do that.' And it turns into a massively successful record for a band that barely exists."

The two musicians worked on the record by mailing their contributions back and forth to each other, Jimmy sending instrumental pieces on a CD-R to Ben, who then added vocals, guitar, and keyboard parts; Jenny Lewis and Jen Wood also provided backing vocals. They chose to release the record under the name the Postal Service, as a jokey reference to how the album came together—a joke that would prove less funny when the United States Postal Service got wind of it.

The group's first single, the wistful "Such Great Heights," was released in January 2003, with an album, *Give Up,* following in February. In order to drum up interest, the single featured the non-album track "There's Never Enough Time" and covers of the band's songs by two other acts, with the Shins covering "We Will Become Silhouettes," and Iron & Wine covering "Such Great Heights." Sub Pop also made what some saw as a controversial decision to offer "Such Great Heights" as a free download from the label's site. It was a decision that helped the song connect in a big way with the growing audience that was now discovering and sharing music online.

"We started getting these insane bandwidth bills from our Internet service provider," Tony recalls. "And we were like, 'What is happening? What could possibly be generating this much traffic?' And we figured out it was hundreds of thousands of downloads of 'Such Great Heights.' Kids had programmed it on their MySpace page to auto-play whenever anybody went to their page, and it would automatically download from our site, which is a real sloppy, old-school, make-it-work, duct tape sort of way to do streaming back in the day. But it was crazy how many people were hearing the song through that."

Right out of the gate, says Tony, the Postal Service became "a crazy big phenomenon." The group's only tour was a sell-out; originally booked in smaller venues, the shows had to be moved to larger halls as the demand for tickets increased. "They did the one tour and then disappeared," says Tony. "But it just kept going." On July 17, 2004, *Give Up* topped *Billboard*'s Top Electronic Albums chart and stayed there for nineteen weeks. "It has surpassed our expectations," Tamborello told the magazine. "We had no ambition to make a crossover album. We didn't even have a plan for an overall sound; we just wanted to make a fun record. We just thought it would find a small audience for people that liked our other bands."

"Such Great Heights," which sold over half a million copies, would eventually be heard in numerous commercials, the TV shows *Grey's Anatomy* and *Veronica Mars*, and the trailer for *Garden State* (with Iron & Wine's cover of the song also appearing on the film's soundtrack). *Give Up* would go on to sell over a million copies, becoming Sub Pop's second-biggest seller, after *Bleach*.

Not everyone was so happy about the band's success. The USPS sent the band a cease-and-desist letter in August 2003, stating that "Postal Service" was a registered trademark. But the dispute was settled amicably by the following year. The USPS allowed the group to continue using the name, in exchange for the band noting USPS's trademark on subsequent releases. The band were also asked to perform at the postmaster general's National Executive Conference in Washington, DC. "It ended up being kind of fun," Jimmy told *Pitchfork*. "It was all very good-natured." The USPS even agreed to sell the CD on its website.

The success of the Shins and the Postal Service fully lifted Sub Pop out of its late-'90s rut. "It's the showbiz adage: nothing succeeds like success," says Jon. "We had a couple of successful artists on the label who in turn inspired other people. The way that we pulled ourselves up was basically getting people in the company who were psyched about their jobs, and working with artists who were genuinely psyched to be on the label. Getting new bands whose deals were more responsible; we weren't paying $150,000 to a band who was a critical favorite but hadn't sold any records. They were artists that were intuitively as in tune to where the company was at the time—that made as much sense to the company at the time as Nirvana and Mudhoney and Soundgarden did in their time. And they were artists who the people working here were actually excited about."

Steve Manning agrees that an influx of new staff had helped rejuvenate the label. "All of the people that had been there in the old days when they had a lot of money and had cushier jobs were gone," he says. "I think at some point in that first year and a half, when we moved out of the Terminal Sales Building, there was a conscious effort made by the staff at that time, mostly new people, to be like, let's just put out records by people we like. Because clearly the label has not been good at picking out great records that will sell. And so the idea is, just go back and put out stuff we like and if it doesn't sell, at least we could stand behind it. So that's when things like the Shins happened, and Iron & Wine happened, and things that really at the time seemed out of the spectrum of what Sub Pop was doing. But it was something we all really believed in, and we liked the people, and liked the music. There was a renewed sense of energy I think that the label had been missing for a while."

For Tony Kiewel, this was the moment when "it felt like all our hard work was paying off. And it felt like we deserved it; it felt like, it's all coming together, we pulled it off, we fucking righted the sinking ship and it felt amazing, honestly. But it also felt like it wasn't just us. That it was our community, right? And we were excited about that. Touch and Go had the Yeah Yeah Yeahs and TV on the Radio, and Merge had Arcade Fire; suddenly it just felt like everybody started to have these bands that were rising up."

◎ ◎ ◎

Sub Pop had felt its artists were unlikely to achieve gold or platinum record award status (sales of half a million or one million copies, respectively), so "wooden record" awards were created, for sales of one hundred thousand copies. "That's indie gold," says Tony. "We felt that was the most you can do without a massive commercial radio hit. But those weren't the rules anymore."

In addition to changes in the musical landscape, there was another change in the industry that was having a far-reaching effect—the rise of the Internet. Sub Pop had readily taken up with the developing technology, beginning in the 1990s.

"Sub Pop made a very concerted effort to be right there with it as the Internet took off," says Dan Trager. "We all had computers, we had email addresses, we had a website. But at the same time, the prevailing notion from the music business was very much head-in-the-sand, denial, and then reactionary. And I remember when Shawn Fanning [co-founder of the file-sharing site Napster] was going on trial, and there were some colleagues that were like, 'Great! I hope they really give it to him!' And I'm thinking, 'I'm not sure this is the right approach.'"

It was easy to make some adjustments; when the Mega Mart closed in 2000, sales were simply moved online, for example. But online music distribution was another matter. Apple opened its iTunes Music Store on April 28, 2003, selling one million songs in the first week. "All of a sudden we had this source of revenue from Apple that we were fascinated by, but we didn't really know what was going to happen with that," says Megan Jasper. "There was a period of time where people used to refer to that as 'free money.' Which made me crazy, coming from a distribution background, because I saw it as digital distribution, and that this could mimic physical distribution, although I would never have guessed that it would've changed as quickly as it ended up changing. But I think because I came from a retail background and was thinking about it in terms of distribution, I could understand that. So I knew it wasn't really 'free money'; it was a different format."

But the success of the Postal Service had revealed that making music available for free could also be beneficial. "We realized two things," says Megan. "One is obvious: word of mouth is the best kind of marketing. But the other things is, giving away music might be a really interesting, smart marketing tool. And so we started thinking, let's give away MP3s. And that became a game changer for us. And I remember a lot of people feeling like we were stupid for doing that; 'Do you really want to give away a song?' I can't tell you how many times we had this conversation. 'We know it seems counterintuitive, but ....' It's like radio. When someone hears something and they really like it and they want to hear it over and over again, they go out and buy the record."

"At the time, it was seen as really radical," says Tony. "I remember having these really intense conversations with bands and managers about why we weren't crazy. Because whatever our priority songs were, we were giving that song away as a download on our site. We just saw it as, people are going to pirate it anyway, so I'd rather they get it from us so that we're in the conversation. And I'd rather control the quality of the song. And also if they like it enough they're going to buy the record. That's the whole point of a single anyway. And we can't get it on the radio, so what are we going to do? But yeah, it was super contentious at the time."

◎ ◎ ◎

As Sub Pop was learning to navigate the new digital realm, the label was also finding success in an unexpected genre—comedy. As Tony had told the *Guardian*, with a Republican administration in office, "American politics were veering sharply to the right. Music had become apolitical, and because of that there wasn't much we could do as a label to participate in the public discourse." But releasing comedy records would allow the label to make their progressive views clear. There were more practical concerns as well: recording a stand-up comic would be inexpensive.

Tony suggested that Sub Pop sign David Cross, who had been working in stand-up comedy since graduating from high school in Atlanta, Georgia; by 1995, he was co-hosting the sketch comedy program *Mr. Show*. "I think we all probably thought it was a long shot, but why not; it could be interesting," says Megan.

Dates on Cross's 2002 US tour were recorded, with the highlights released that November, as the album *Shut Up, You Fucking Baby!* Cross's routines made it clear where his political sympathies lay. "I'm not saying that all Republicans are racist, sexist homophobes," he said on his second Sub Pop album, *That's Not Funny* (2004), "Just the people they choose to elect into office."

*Shut Up, You Fucking Baby!* received a Grammy nomination for "Best Comedy Album"—a first for Sub Pop. Through Cross, the company was introduced to other comedians, and soon the roster featured such performers as Eugene Mirman (*En Garde, Society!*, 2006; *God Is a Twelve-Year-Old Boy with Asperger's*, 2009), Patton Oswalt (*Werewolves and Lollipops*, 2007), and, later, Sarah Silverman (*We Are Miracles*, 2014), and Jon Benjamin (*Well, I Should Have...\**, 2015).

And then came New Zealand comedy duo Jemaine Clement and Bret McKenzie, who worked under the name Flight of the Conchords. The two met while attending Victoria University of Wellington and first worked together in the 1990s, in the comedy troupe So You're a Man. By the end of the decade, the two had formed Flight of the Conchords, making their television debut in 2000 and releasing their first album, *Folk the World Tour*, in 2002. By 2005, they had a self-titled BBC radio series revolving around their attempts to find success in London. A similar theme provided the premise for their subsequent HBO TV series, set in New York City, which began its two-season run in 2007.

It was at this time that the duo were picked up by Sub Pop, when their manager, Mike Martinovich, sent Jon, whom he knew, some of the Conchords' material. As it happened, Jon had a keen interest in New Zealand, having visited the country numerous times, and even flying Sub Pop's entire staff down for a visit. "I remember Jonathan saying, 'Mike Martinovich sent this over, it's two comics from New Zealand,'" says Megan. "I think he saw 'New Zealand,' and he was so thrilled that something came from New Zealand. He said, 'Listen to it and see if you're into it.' It was a video, and a bunch of us put it on in the conference room and we all were laughing. They were charming, and they were funny, and they were so good at what they were doing. And it turned out that some of our comedian friends knew them and loved them, and it just felt like a perfect fit."

The Conchords' first release on Sub Pop would be *The Distant Future*, released in 2007, featuring three songs from the HBO series and two live tracks. The record won the Grammy for "Best Comedy Album" the following year. Given Sub Pop's history of pranks and over-the-top hyperbole, it was perhaps appropriate that the company's first major award would be for a comedy record—though it was also ironic, considering how Sub Pop had made its name championing bands from the Pacific Northwest, that the label's first act to win a Grammy wasn't even from the United States. The duo would release two more records on Sub Pop: *Flight of the Conchords* (2008), which reached no. 3 on the *Billboard* 200; and *I Told You I Was Freaky* (2009), which reached no. 19; both albums also topped *Billboard*'s comedy chart.

There was also an old favorite that returned to the label: Mudhoney. Reprise had dropped the band after the release of *Tomorrow Hit Today* in 1998. Bassist Matt Lukin then announced he wanted to quit, and Mudhoney's future was suddenly in limbo. But after the release of the *March to Fuzz* compilation, drummer Dan Peters ran into Jon, who said Sub Pop would be interested in a new album by the group.

The remaining members eventually brought in Guy Maddison, whom they knew from Australian band Lubricated Goat, to replace Lukin. Guy now lived in Seattle, where he worked as a nurse; he'd also played in one of Mark Arm's side project bands, Bloodloss. *Since We've Become Translucent* was released on Sub Pop in 2002, and Mudhoney have remained on the label ever since. Mark Arm's day job is also at Sub Pop: he's the manager of the label's warehouse, overseeing the company's mail orders.

And after years of estrangement, Bruce too had "come home," in a sense. He had finally sold his shares in Sub Pop: "Essentially, the finalization of a divorce," he says. It helped clear the air, and he and Jon began to enjoy a more congenial relationship. In 2003, he was invited to DJ at the label's anniversary party, held on April 27 at the Crocodile. He was later taken on by the label as a consultant. "It meant that in exchange for occasional opinions, I would be invited to their annual Christmas outings, which included year-end meetings," he explains. "I would also participate in any interview requests that the label might have. It was a tough gig!"

By 2005, Jon clearly felt Sub Pop was back on solid ground. "I'm not saying that I'm a business maven by any stretch—quite the contrary," he said in an interview with me at the time. "But at this point, after having made every mistake that there is to make, I do have the ability of learning from my mistakes. Now, everything is very carefully planned. There is room for spontaneity; if we hear an artist that we want to work with, we go for it. But we have budgets, and lots of meetings, and a lot of consensus building, and all the things that really did not exist at all in the early days of Sub Pop. And my guess would be that the music companies are trying to become more like Sub Pop, from the standpoint that I think that we're able to operate with small staffs and pretty tight budgets. To that extent, I think that the larger music companies are trying to be more like us."

◎ ◎ ◎

That same year, Sub Pop moved again, to its current location, back downtown at 2013 Fourth Avenue. A secured entry to the building meant no one was going to wander in off the street looking to buy a sandwich, though receptionist Derek Erdman, in an article for the *Stranger*, did note the occasional trespass, such as a man who'd got inside and "handed me his demo CD with a hand covered in oozing sores."

"Luckily, these things don't happen *every* day," he added.

The Sub Pop staff had learned how to run the company in a more fiscally responsible fashion, keeping an eye on the budget. Now, the label began looking at how to run the company in a more socially responsible way as well, and in 2006, Sub Pop became the first record label to be Green-e certified. Kelley Stoltz's *Below the Branches*, released by Sub Pop in February 2006, was the first album to be entirely recorded using renewable energy. Stoltz tracked his energy usage during the making of his album, then offset it by purchasing Green Tags (also known as Renewable Energy Certificates). "This ensures that every kilowatt-hour of electricity drawn from the grid to power Kelley's equipment is replaced with an equal amount of non-polluting renewable energy," Sub Pop explained on its blog.

The company then decided to have Sub Pop start using renewable energy itself, and on July 29, a press release was issued stating that the label had purchased enough Green-e certified Green Tags to cover 100 percent of the company's energy use. "I was made aware of the program by one of my co-workers," Jon was quoted as saying. "I was, quite frankly, shocked by how easy it is to support renewable energy. Green Tags are a simple way for anyone to choose wind energy, which, in turn, lowers dependence on burning fossils fuels for energy. Green Tags fulfill an important commitment to both the planet and the Pacific Northwest, where Sub Pop is rooted."

In 2007, Sub Pop started another imprint: Hardly Art. The label's previous subsidiary, Die Young Stay Pretty, had only released records by three bands (the Murder City Devils, the Black Halos, and Track Star), and had shut down in 1999, when Meg Watjen, who ran the label, left the company.

"One of the things that both Tony and Jon do an awful lot is pitch bands," says Megan. "And at some point, they were pitching enough bands, along with other people at the label, to where we were saying no to artists that we didn't want to say no to. And so I remember at one point Jonathan was like, 'We need another label.' And we realized maybe this is the time to do that."

They were also keen to "experiment with a different business model," Tony explains. "At the time, Sub Pop did traditional, almost major label–style royalty deals. At Hardly Art, we decided from the very beginning we were going to do net profit splits. We were going to do things like pure 50/50 [splits], we were going to do one-off deals; we really just wanted to make it as artist friendly as possible, and lower budget. It also felt like, 'You know what? The rules are changing, and this is an opportunity to not just experiment with these deal parameters, but also with different ways of doing business.' And maybe this is a result of having experimented with it at Hardly Art, but more often than not, we're doing net profit split deals on the Sub Pop side now, too."

Sarah Moody, one of Sub Pop's publicists, was made general manager of Hardly Art, the label's name taken from a lyric in the song "No Culture Icons" by Portland band the Thermals (who recorded their first three albums for Sub Pop). The label's first record was *In Camera*, by Seattle duo Arthur & Yu, released in June 2007.

Hardly Art wasn't meant to be a farm team for Sub Pop but instead to become a label in its own right. "Our first goal was to just to have another place that we could put artists that we love," says Megan. "And then we realized, no, it can't just be for overflow, there has to be something that feels different. We need to give it room so it can be its own thing, and not just be 'Sub Pop Junior.' We developed it with the hope of being able to engage artists that we were turning away before. But it quickly became its own thing, where it wasn't for overflow."

With its smaller budgets and overheads (three people run the label), Hardly Art was better able to work with emerging bands—acts that wouldn't generate the kind of revenue needed to release a record on Sub Pop but could turn a profit on a smaller label—the kind of label that Sub Pop itself used to be.

◎ ◎ ◎

The Shins' third album, *Wincing the Night Away*, was released in January 2007. It debuted at no. 2 on the *Billboard* 200—making it still the highest-charting Sub Pop record ever—and sold over a million copies. The Shins broke another barrier when they became the first Sub Pop band to appear on the popular late night TV programs *Late Show with David Letterman* and *Saturday Night Live*.

"It was amazing," Steve Manning says. "It really was amazing. Sub Pop had never had an artist on *Letterman* before; they'd only had one *Last Call with Carson Daly* thing prior to that. But the Shins changed the perception of booking agents at the television shows about having truly independent artists on. When the Shins were on *Saturday Night Live*, they were the first truly independent label band to be on *Saturday Night Live*. I felt like it was a breakthrough in the industry to have these kinds of artists getting these kinds of opportunities. And I think they can be thought of as an artist that opened a lot of doors for people. And while I was at Sub Pop, we ended up doing forty TV appearances for artists over that time. So we went from zero to it becoming a regular part of what we were doing."

Over the preceding nineteen years, Sub Pop had endured the kinds of blows that might have felled a lesser label. But now, on the verge of going into its third decade, it was still standing.

# 7
# HOLDING STEADY

*The fact that our business is in pretty good shape right now has
a lot to do with having experienced prolonged anxiety at living
on the edge. Which is something I don't ever want to do again.*

—Jon Poneman, "Spirit of '88," *Mojo*, August 2008

MEMORANDUM
TO: Everyone
FROM: Sub Pop Records
DATE: April 2, 2008
SUBJECT: World domination
Mission complete.
JP/cmn

So read the press release issued to commemorate Sub Pop's twentieth
anniversary. The three-page document was surprisingly frank about the
difficulties the company had faced over the years and how they'd been
overcome: "Outrageous advances for bands and videos have been scrapped.
Sub Pop works to make its bands as self-sufficient as possible. Tours are
designed to make money, rather than be artificially buoyed by the label.
Realistic recording budgets are set so bands have a chance to earn royalties
even on modest sales."

Along with a timeline and a list of notable releases was a sheet entitled "Sub
Pop, by the Numbers," offering an array of fun factoids:

Most releases by a single artist ...... 17, Mudhoney
Number of releases through June 2008 ...... 777
Free downloads of the Postal Service's "Such Great Heights" on
subpop.com ...... 11,655,300
Employees as of March 2008 ...... 27
Dogs roaming the halls of Sub Pop HQ ...... 3
Cost in cents for a 12 oz. Rainier Beer in lunch room soda machine ...... 75
Corporate charitable donations in US dollars for 2007 ...... $250,000

The big anniversary event for 2008 was the SP20 festival, at that time
the biggest celebration in the label's history. All the performers appeared for
free; proceeds were pooled together and divided among the acts, who then
designated a specific charity to receive the funds. Green River and Mudhoney
donated their share to the Northwest Parkinson's Foundation; Red Red Meat
chose the Accelerated Cure Project (benefiting multiple sclerosis research);
the Vaselines chose the Bellur Trust (benefiting the children of Bellur, India);
Iron & Wine chose the Foundation for the Advancement of Midwifery;
Flight of the Conchords chose the Red Cross International Response Fund.
In 2010, a nineteen-track album documenting the event was released, *SP20:
Casual Nostalgia Fest*; proceeds were earmarked for the Clinton Bush Haiti
Fund (a nonprofit formed by former presidents Bill Clinton and George
W. Bush, raising funds for the victims of the earthquake that hit Haiti on
January 12, 2010).

The twentieth anniversary was also commemorated by the return of the Sub
Pop Singles Club, the second edition of the club having come to an end in 2002,
with the release of Ugly Casanova's "Diggin' Holes"/ "Baby's Clean Conscience"
(thirteen hundred copies on clear yellow vinyl). "It went away for the same
reasons it went away the first time: declining membership, fewer artists that
we actually wanted to do singles with," says Jon. "It was a diminishing returns

proposition. It came back because there were a lot of people at the label who were sort of Sub Pop sentimentalists and they were like, 'We think these are cool and we think the label started to suck when you got rid of the Singles Club.' So I was like, 'You know what? Bring it back. If there's a lot of bands you want to work with, if you want to oversee it, then let's do it.' But very quickly it became evident that it was a hassle."

When it was announced that the Singles Club would be relaunched in August 2008, it was made clear that it would be for a limited time only: one year, "before returning to its secret island vacation spot for eternity (or until we here at Sub Pop feel masochistic enough to take on coordinating this debacle again)," as the official announcement put it. For $75 ($90 if mailed outside of North America), subscribers would receive twelve singles pressed in limited-edition runs of fifteen hundred copies, which would also include a free download. "So here's your chance to join the throngs of assholes selling their collectibles on eBay for ridiculous sums!" the announcement concluded. "All you have to do is: SEND US YOUR MONEY!" The first single, released in August 2008, was "Gebel Barkal"/ "(Version)" by San Francisco band Om.

The year also saw the release of Mudhoney's *Superfuzz Bigmuff: Deluxe Edition*. Sub Pop had already reissued many of its previous releases, primarily by upgrading vinyl records to CDs. These were generally straightforward reissues, though when *Bleach* was reissued in 1992, it was remastered, and some other album reissues featured non-album singles. But the company was increasingly aware of its role in rock history, and it began giving key releases notable upgrades. The *Superfuzz Bigmuff* reissue featured the original album plus non-album singles, compilation tracks, and live performances, including the band's first overseas appearance at the Berlin Independence Days Festival in 1988. The 2009 Deluxe Edition of *Bleach* featured a previously unreleased live show from 1990. Over the years, Red Red Meat's *Bunny Gets Paid*, Sebadoh's *Bakesale*, and Wolf Parade's *Apologies to the Queen Mary*, among others, have all come in for the "Deluxe Edition" treatment.

The company also began issuing expanded packages of records it hadn't originally released. In 2017, the label re-released Soundgarden's *Ultramega OK*, which had originally been issued by SST in 1988. The original album was remixed, and the set also included early versions of a number of tracks. The same year also saw the release of *U-Men*, a two-CD retrospective bringing together all the tracks the band recorded between 1984 and 1989 (including their first EP, released on Bruce's Bombshelter Records label), along with some rarities.

Jack Endino was brought in to work on a number of the reissues. "I'm like the reissue guy at this point," he says. "They give me the archival work, starting with supervising the remastering of *Screaming Life* [reissued in 2013] and stuff like that." He welcomed the chance to revisit, and sometimes improve, records he'd previously worked on. "It's quite enjoyable. Because, quite frankly, a lot of them were done on the cheap, in a hurry, without a lot of attention being put into the sound, really. And also, we didn't have the experience or the time or the money. And now, with 20/20 hindsight, I can go back and go, 'Oh, God! That thing is actually really murky! We could make that sound a little better now if we did a fresh digital transfer of it, and had new converters, better sounding pre-amplifiers, and so forth. Let's try it.' And you do it, and then you go, 'Oh my God, this sounds way better than I remember it; why don't we make the record and the CD reflect how good it sounds?'

"Digital mastering in 1999, 1998, was very much in its infancy. And early CDs really don't sound very good. Some of the original vinyl sounds okay, but some of the original CDs from that era are really pretty wretched sounding. But being able to go back and revisit that—you can do terrible damage to a record if you're not careful. I was very, very meticulous with the remastering of *Bleach*, with how George Morino [credited with mastering the reissue] approached it, which was to make it sound good, and not make it sound stupid and squashed and compressed."

There was an altruistic enterprise launched in 2008 as well: the Sub Pop Scholarship, announced in March. It offered three scholarships (one for $6,000, two for $3,500), to be awarded to students bound for college who were interested in music and/or the creative arts. Applicants were asked to submit an essay, along with examples of their artwork. Suggested topics for the essay included such expected queries as "What are you doing in the arts/music field in your community?" and "What are your influences and/or who inspires you?" By 2018, the scholarship fund had increased to $15,000 (one award for $7,000, one for $5,000, and one for $3,000), and the questions had broadened to "How has your family or community background affected the way you see the world?" and the decidedly jocular, "What does being a Sub Pop 'Loser' mean to you?"

Of all the articles written about Sub Pop over the years, not many have mentioned one important aspect of the company's operations that's grown since the label has become more solvent and financially stable: its commitment to being both progressive and socially responsible. In the early years, when an employee's paycheck might bounce, it wasn't possible for the company to give back to the community financially (though Sub Pop's bands regularly played benefit shows). Today, giving back to the community is very much a part of Sub Pop's philosophy, and is something the label does through various means: donations, scholarships, having a page on the company's website recommending specific charities, looking for more green-friendly ways to do business, and encouraging voter registration through postcards written in the company's own inimitable style ("Dearest Loser, Did you know that 45 percent of adults who live in the US did not participate on election day 2016?").

Megan Jasper sees this as a reflection of the Sub Pop staff's own values. "I would say that the majority of us who work here care so much about the city and the world that we live in. A lot of us do volunteer work; a lot of us are on boards or commissions. I feel like we walk the walk as individuals, and as a company, if we didn't do that, it would feel like a poor reflection of integrity. And I think that we are a proud group, and we want to feel proud. And doing those things, pushing for progress, that makes us feel proud."

But she also sees the desire to "push for progress" as something that comes naturally to those who grew up feeling like outsiders. "We grew up in Loserville," she says. "We grew up wearing those 'LOSER' shirts. And the reason why that resonated with us is because so many of us were just misfits growing up. We didn't have a place. You're never a cool kid when you grow up feeling like a misfit. But when you can become comfortable in your own skin and you can own it, and you can wear your differences and the things that make you *you*, proudly, that's ultimately I think what 'cool' is. Being comfortable being yourself, and being good to people at the same time.

"But you don't know that when you're young. You just feel like you fit in, or you don't fit in. And if you can find a group of people who accept you for who you are, I think it makes you want to push for what you see as progress. You want the world to be okay for people, you want the world to be okay for young people, you want them to learn different lessons than you had to learn. So I think that plays into what we do as a company, and I think that's how we express it."

Jon has a similar perspective. "I have a fundamental belief that Bruce and I created something here that is—it's like community outreach," he says. "Bruce and I, when we worked at Muzak, both had the experience of being at the bottom of a top-down organization. I mean, it was like *Bonfire of the Vanities*, that sort of exaggerated '80s Wall Street–esque, caricatures of the

'Masters of the Universe'–type thing. In creating our company, we wanted it to be successful. But we wanted everybody to be respected, everybody to be heard—a real emphasis on collaboration, a real emphasis on community. The idea, particularly for me, was to create a place where it's basically a safe haven for people who felt brutalized by that other world.

"And there's so many of us out there who come from the same place. And so many of them want the same thing. And Sub Pop has been successful because we work with great bands, and because we are in a great community, and we have great people, but all of this exists in a philosophical and moral commitment to collaboration. And my optimism comes from my belief in the collaborative environment that is Sub Pop. And that by simply enduring, we are able to breathe life into and participate in the much bigger collaborative effort—which is civilization.

"That may have been a little bit of a stretch," he concludes with a laugh. "Maybe the five-block radius surrounding the Marshall Building in downtown Seattle [where the Sub Pop offices are located]. But you get my point."

◎ ◎ ◎

After so many years of unrest, this was a stable period for the label. There were no sudden runaway successes like the Postal Service. But there was plenty of excitement over new groups, like the acoustic/folk-influenced Fleet Foxes. The founding members of the group, Robin Pecknold and Skyler Skjelset, had been playing music together since meeting at Lake Washington High School in Kirkland, a Seattle suburb. Post-high school, the band generated attention by playing area clubs and sharing music via their MySpace page.

The group had recorded an album's worth of material, but had yet to release it when they signed with Sub Pop; their first release for the label ended up being an EP, *Sun Giant*, recorded after work on their debut album had been completed. *Sun Giant* was released in April 2008; the album, *Fleet Foxes*, followed in June. The layered vocal harmonies and folk-pop generated immediate acclaim. "Six months ago, Fleet Foxes were just another aspiring band quietly plying their trade on MySpace," wrote the *Independent*. "Now, they are 2008's must-hear act."

*Fleet Foxes* cracked the *Billboard* Top 40 and sold over four hundred thousand copies in the US (in the UK, where the album was released on the Bella Union label, it reached the Top 5). "As a musical accomplishment, it's hard for me to think of a record that we've put out that surpasses this record," Jon told *Spin*. "Even if they were to stop now, this is a career-defining work." The band's next album, 2011's *Helplessness Blues*, received a Grammy nomination for "Best Folk Album." It was also partly recorded at a studio that had a long history with Sub Pop: Reciprocal Recording.

Seattle band the Head and the Heart mined a similar indie-folk terrain. The six members of the group had met at open mic night at Seattle's Conor Byrne Pub in 2009. That same year, they released their debut, self-titled album themselves; it became a local hit, eventually selling over ten thousand copies. Sub Pop signed the band and re-released the debut in April 2011, remastering the album, re-recording "Sounds Like Hallelujah," and adding a studio version of "Rivers and Roads."

It was a wise move. "Rivers and Roads," a melancholy song of romantic yearning, was quickly picked up for use in such television shows as *Chuck*, *How I Met Your Mother*, and *New Girl*. The band's songs would eventually appear in a number of TV shows, film trailers, and movies—an increasingly lucrative market for music acts. *The Head and the Heart* went on to sell over half a million copies; not only did it reach no. 3 in *Billboard*'s Folk Albums chart, it crossed over into the magazine's many other charts as well: Rock Albums (no.

23), Alternative Albums (no. 18), and Independent Albums (no. 14). The band's second album, 2013's *Let's Be Still*, peaked at no. 10 on the *Billboard* 200 chart, topped the Folk Albums chart, and sold over two hundred thousand copies. The title track was featured in a commercial for Corona beer.

Sub Pop also began expanding its roster of hip-hop acts, beginning with the release of Shabazz Palaces' *Black Up* in 2011. (The label had signed its first hip-hop group, the Evil Tambourines, in 1999.) The group was a duo of Ishmael Butler and Tendai "Baba" Maraire. Ishmael, born in Seattle, had moved to Massachusetts to attend college, then dropped out and moved to Brooklyn to pursue a career in music. In the late '80s, he co-founded Digable Planets; the group's 1992 single "Rebirth of Slick (Cool Like Dat)" won the Grammy for "Best Rap Performance by a Duo or Group."

The group broke up in 1995, and in 2003 Ishmael returned to Seattle to look after his mother. By then, he'd also given up music. Then Tendai, who'd been involved with music since he was a child and had performed as a rapper named Boy Wonder, asked Ishmael about working together. With Tendai handling the instrumentation, and Ishmael as the duo's vocalist, Shabazz Palaces (with Ishmael crediting himself as Palaceer Lazaro) self-released two EPs in 2009 and a live album in 2010.

By that time, Sub Pop had become interested. "Shabazz Palaces was already getting a lot of attention in Seattle when we started talking to them, and there were a number of fans in the office," says Tony Kiewel. "We had a relationship with their manager at the time, Jonathan Moore, who had worked with Band of Horses [who recorded two albums for Sub Pop]. From the start, they were more interested in working with a strong local company of people they liked than in connecting with a label that perhaps had more experience with hip-hop. And for Sub Pop, working with incredibly talented artists based in Seattle is the most natural thing in the world."

"*Black Up* is a lesson in forceful insolence," wrote the *New Yorker* on the album's release, "stocked with music that rests in the low end, only to be unpredictably split apart by noise." The album also ended up on numerous critics' "best of" lists in 2011. *Black Up* was followed by *Lese Majesty* in 2014, and a joint release, *Quazarz: Born on a Gangster Star* and *Quazarz vs. the Jealous Machines, in 2017, the latter two concerning the journey of* "Quazarz," an extraterrestrial who visits earth and observes life in the "United States of Amurderca." Ishmael attributed the "trippy creativity" of his work to Seattle's natural environment, telling the *New York Times*, "It's, like, mystical, with the rain and mountains and the fresh water and the salt water and the hills."

In 2013, Ishmael became an A&R rep for Sub Pop. Soon, other hip-hop acts were being signed, such as Seattle's THEESatisfaction and South Africa's Spoek Mathambo. In 2014, Sub Pop released *CLPPNG*, the debut album by experimental rap group clipping. A Sub Pop co-worker who had shared a bill with the group sent Tony a link to the trio's music on Bandcamp, a music distribution site. "I had never heard a band like them before," he says. "They were influenced in equal measures by experimental noise groups, avant-garde composers, and East Bay rap. They sounded new and dangerous and exciting. I flew down to LA and saw them play at The Smell to a packed room of teenage kids moshing."

The group was comprised of rapper Daveed Diggs (who would win a Tony and a Grammy for his joint performance as Thomas Jefferson/Marquis de Lafayette in *Hamilton*), and producers William Hutson and Jonathan Snipes. Their second album, *Splendor and Misery*, set its story in the future, the tale of a slave in the cargo hold of a space ship. The record's science-fiction theme led to it being nominated for a Hugo Award for "Best Dramatic Presentation, Short Form." It was a rare honor for a music group; the last musician to receive a Hugo nomination had been Paul Kantner, the guitarist in Jefferson Airplane/ Jefferson Starship, for his 1970 album *Blows Against the Empire*.

◎ ◎ ◎

Sub Pop also continued to learn to adapt to the ever-changing ways music was being distributed. "There's a lot of trial and error," says Tony. "And even then, whatever actually works doesn't work for more than a month anyway. I think a lot of it is being flexible. That's something that Jon and Megan have always been really emphatic about; that one of our strengths to keep as a core value, if we're going to survive, is being nimble."

Spotify, a streaming service, launched on October 7, 2008, and in the years since, music listeners have increasingly moved to such platforms. "Now nobody even wants downloads, they just want to stream stuff," Tony agrees. "There's a fundamental difference in the reason why someone buys a record now. Nobody hears a song on the radio and likes it, and goes to a store and buys a CD. Which is totally what I would've done in high school. No way, does not happen anymore.

"What a record, and a CD, is to a customer or a music fan, is a token of fandom. Maybe there's some people who, for audiophile reasons, want to enjoy it on that particular format, but that is probably a single-digit percentage of our customers. The vast majority of them are buying a thing because they already know they like the album, and they're almost just voting for it. And more often than not, our anecdotal research seems to indicate that even after they buy the record, they're not listening to the record—they're still listening to it on Spotify. And the people who pre-order the record are people who want a collectible edition of it, our 'Loser' editions, or they're a hardcore fan and they want to be in there and demonstrate their fandom. But again, very few of them are rolling the dice; they've already decided they like it for some reason."

This calls for a new kind of strategy to get people to buy a recording: "wrapping your head around this fundamental disconnect between experiencing the music and buying the record," says Tony. "If they don't experience the music first, they're not going to buy the record. I think understanding that is the beginning place of being able to sell them the record. And that's what we were doing when we were giving away the MP3s, without necessarily 100 percent understanding that there had been a societal shift in the thinking. Because it hadn't really happened yet. It's more that now, with Spotify, that that's the case. Back then, it was just that there's piracy and people were starting to engage in trading MP3s online and stuff. But it still makes total sense to me now, that that's why things are the way they are. So now the goal is, how do I become part of the conversation?"

On the verge of the label's twenty-fifth anniversary, Sub Pop was still finding new ways to become a part of the conversation.

# 8
# GOING SILVER

*We're not the best, but we're pretty good.*

—Company motto, SubPop.com

Sub Pop upped the ante for its silver anniversary in 2013. In 2008, a Sub Pop flag had flown from the top of the Space Needle. Now, on July 11, 2013, it was Mudhoney themselves atop the Needle—not flying in the breeze, but playing a ten-song set. It was a perfect choice; no other band on Sub Pop's roster would so aptly fit the bill. "Apart from being Sub Pop's prodigal sons, they are and forever will be Sub Pop's flagship band, spiritually," Jon told *Rolling Stone*.

The idea was Megan Jasper's. "I called the Space Needle to see if they'd be willing to do something with us," she recalls. "I spoke with [director of publicity] Dave Mandapat who told me to 'think big' and not just pitch waving our flag again; we should try to think of something that hadn't been done before. I asked if it might be possible to have a band play outside on the top of the Needle to which he responded, 'That's exactly what I'm talking about!' At the same time, KEXP had been talking with the Space Needle about doing a live broadcast, and so we all partnered up and made it happen."

The result was a daylong celebration in advance of Sub Pop's Silver Jubilee festival, which was being held that weekend. Jon and Megan were interviewed at KEXP's offices in the morning, then, at noon, the station switched to a live broadcast from the Space Needle's Observation Deck, mixing interviews with Bruce Pavitt, Kim Thayil, and Jack Endino with live performances by J. Mascis (the Dinosaur Jr. vocalist/guitarist had released a solo album, *Tied to a Star*, on Sub Pop) and Sera Cahoone.

At 5 p.m., Mudhoney's set began, and was streamed live by the station. They opened with—what else?—"Touch Me I'm Sick." Given the space restrictions, Mark refrained from his more kinetic stage movements and body contortions. Nor did he play guitar, leading the *Mudhoney Tourbook* website to meticulously note it was the first known performance of "Into the Drink" and "Suck You Dry" done in such a fashion, and the second known performance of "Touch Me I'm Sick" and "Who You Drivin' Now?" without Mark's guitar licks. "This became only the second show that the guys performed where they were all completely sober," the website added (the other being a "Rock the Vote" benefit show on the UCLA campus that started at noon on March 5, 1992).

Megan and Bruce were among the select few who were allowed on top of the Space Needle to watch the performance as it happened, an experience Megan called "a mind blow, totally amazing, and completely surreal." "It was one of the greatest shows of my life—and I've seen a few," says Bruce. "The band had come a long way since I saw their first show at the Vogue with Das Damen in April of '88." After being interviewed by KEXP earlier in the day, Charles Peterson had the daunting assignment of photographing the show from a helicopter, which circled around the band as he precariously hung out of the door. In 2014, the vinyl album *KEXP Presents Mudhoney Live on Top of the Space Needle* was released on Record Store Day.

The Mudhoney show was one of a number of things Sub Pop had put together to celebrate its twenty-fifth anniversary. April had seen the release of two limited-edition compilations. The first, *Sub Pop 1000*, a compilation of previously unreleased songs by Lori Goldston (the cellist on Nirvana's *Unplugged* performance), husband-and-wife duo Peaking Lights, and Detroit's Protomartyr, among others, was issued on limited-edition vinyl and as a download. There was also a compilation CD, *The Silver Ticket*, a sampler drawn from Sub Pop's current roster, including the Ruby Suns, King Tuff, and Father John Misty (aka Joshua Tillman, formerly the drummer in Fleet Foxes). There was also a previously unreleased version of Shabazz Palaces' "Recollections of the Wraith," remixed by the Helio Sequence. As a portrait of Sub Pop in 2013, both releases showed a label in good health, celebrating the present and looking forward to the future more than resting on the laurels of past accomplishments.

Next, the Sub Pop Mega Mart made a temporary return, with a pop-up Mega Mart opening on June 8 in Seattle's Georgetown neighborhood. The front room of the storefront was set up like a living room, with couches, a record player, and board games for people who wanted to come in and hang out. The main space, described as "a wonderland of records and merchandise" by the *Stranger*, also had an entire wall covered with an installation assembled by Jeff Kleinsmith, Sub Pop's senior art director, and Sasha Barr, the label's art director, featuring ephemera from Sub Pop's archives: posters, press releases, and the original layout board for the artwork of Nirvana's "Sliver" single.

The main event was the Silver Jubilee festival, billed as a twenty-fifth anniversary "public display of affection," or, as Megan more colorfully put it to *Rolling Stone*, "a big-ass fuckin' party that'll be really, really fun." First, on July 12, came "Silver Jubil-eve: A 25th Anniversary Comedy Thing (for Charity!)." The show was hosted by Eugene Mirman, with performances by Marc Maron, Jon Benjamin, Kristen Schaal, and Kurt Braunohler, and was held at the Moore Theatre. Maron was best known for his podcast *WTF with Marc Maron*; Mirman, Benjamin, Schaal, and Braunohler had all lent their voices to the animated series *Bob's Burgers*, which began airing in 2011. Sub Pop would later release an album of music from the show.

The Silver Jubilee itself, a free event, was held on July 13 in Georgetown, coinciding with the neighborhood's Georgetown Second Saturday Art Attack, ensuring a robust turnout; proceeds would benefit Northwest Harvest, the Northwest Parkinson's Foundation, and KEXP. Jon was especially pleased that the event was being held in Seattle. "Marymoor Park was wonderful," he told *Seattle Metropolitan.* "But Sub Pop has a particular attachment to Seattle proper—not to the Eastside. So we wanted to choose a neighborhood that we felt maintained the spirit of the Seattle from which Sub Pop sprang. Georgetown was the logical place to go."

There were four stages, including one dedicated solely to Hardly Art bands, with performances running for a full twelve hours, beginning with Shearwater (from Austin, Texas) and closing with the Moondoggies (from Everett, Washington). There was a record fair, featuring vendors representing seventeen other Northwest record labels in addition to Sub Pop. In the beer garden, the Elysian Brewing Company not only served up pints of Loser Pale Ale, but also two other music-themed brews: Nevermind Pale Ale ("An easy-drinking, not at all grungy pale ale. 5.8 percent ABV") and Superfuzz Blood Orange Pale Ale ("Pale ale bursting with blood orange and Citra hops. 5.4 percent ABV"). Crowds filled the Mega Mart all day; according to manager Tim Hayes (who'd owned Fallout Records from 1999 to 2003), records by Mudhoney and Fleet Foxes were the most popular. After dark, there was a screening of *Dazed and Confused.* In a nod to the past, Jack Endino, fronting his group Endino's Earthworm, wore a "What Part Of WE DON'T HAVE ANY MONEY Don't You Understand?" T-shirt.

Bruce could be found on a panel, "Pop Goes Seattle: The Seminal Years of Sub Pop," at the Fantagraphics Bookstore & Gallery, which also included Charles Peterson, cartoonist Peter Bagge, and musician/novelist Danny Bland. The panelists were seated in front of a wall displaying more Sub Pop memorabilia.

For Bruce, the Silver Jubilee festival "was completely surreal. Completely surreal. There were an estimated forty thousand people in Georgetown. I thought it was very well executed. I thought Sub Pop did an excellent job orchestrating that. To me, the most surreal moment was when [Seattle mayor] Mike McGinn rode up on his bicycle wearing a Sub Pop T-shirt. It was, 'All right—thing's getting weird.' The label's had a longstanding reputation for certain levels of hype, and I seriously don't think they can top what happened on the twenty-fifth. I think they should just put it to bed and say, 'We're never going to throw another party as long as we live.'"

For Jon, the Silver Jubilee was "the third best day of my life, behind getting born and getting married."

◎ ◎ ◎

The good spirits that the Silver Jubilee generated were much needed at this time. A few months previously, Jon had gone public with some sad news: he'd been diagnosed with Parkinson's disease. He'd received the diagnosis back in 2010 and finally spoke openly about it to *Seattle Times* columnist Nicole Brodeur, who wrote a sympathetic piece that appeared in the paper on May 31, 2013. Despite what the paper called a "dire diagnosis," Jon remained positive. "You have these morbid thoughts," he admitted. "Then you realize that if things are going to go away, they are not going to go away immediately … My love of life and its precious elements became more vivid at the thought of seeing them fade away." He had no plans to stop working; instead, he'd set up a stationary bike in his office so he could exercise his legs. "I accept that I have this disease," he said elsewhere in the article, "but that doesn't give me the right to be passive."

He certainly wasn't hesitant about continuing his duties as the primary public face of Sub Pop. Post-Silver Jubilee, Jon was next seen being crowned "King Neptune" for Seafair, a summer festival in Seattle that included numerous neighborhood events, as well as a grand Torchlight Parade, a hydroplane race, and an aerial show by the Blue Angels. "Though Seafair is not something I paid attention to—other than Blue Angels flying above and getting into traffic jams around the parade and stuff like that—it is a Seattle institution," he told *Seattle Metropolitan*. "And I am nothing if not a proud Seattle resident. If this is a duty that comes with being that, I embrace it proudly. It'll be fun."

There were other local honors as well. On April 9, 2014, a new plaque was unveiled on the "Seattle Walk of Fame" around the main Nordstrom store in downtown Seattle. The plaque featured Bruce and Jon's footprints (a pair of Blundstone boots and Nike sneakers, respectively) with their signatures in bronze underneath. "Since 1988, Sub Pop Records has lifted many Seattle-area musicians from local obscurity to international acclaim," read the accompanying description. "Proud to claim Seattle as its hometown, Sub Pop has left an enduring legacy in the Pacific Northwest and beyond."

Both Jon and Bruce made some remarks at the unveiling. In addition to thanking the Nordstrom family and their own families and friends, Jon jokingly thanked "all of our creditors" and "anyone who has ever blown their paycheck at www.subpop.com." Humorously, their plaque was placed next to that of a purveyor of a more decorous musical form: Gerald Schwartz, the former music director of the Seattle Symphony. Just down the block is a plaque for mountain climbers Jim and Lou Whittaker; Jim is the father of Bob Whittaker, Mudhoney's manager.

The following day, Nirvana became the first Sub Pop–affiliated act to be inducted into the Rock and Roll Hall of Fame, twenty years after Kurt Cobain's death. Bruce had published his own Nirvana-related tribute the previous year, *Experiencing Nirvana: Grunge in Europe, 1989*, featuring pictures he'd taken of the Nirvana/TAD European tour, as well as the December 1989 Lame Fest show in London with Mudhoney. "I call it a micro history because it just deals with eight days in the lives of these three bands," he says. "But it's a pretty pivotal time for three Seattle bands to go to London and play a sold-out music showcase in front of the British music elite and kill it." In 2014, he went back into his personal archives again, publishing *Sub Pop USA: The Subterranean Pop Music Anthology, 1980–1988*, which reproduced all his *Subterranean Pop/ Sub Pop* fanzines, and every single "Sub Pop U.S.A." column he'd written for *The Rocket*—an invaluable documentation of Sub Pop's early years.

There was one shop certain to carry Bruce's books. On May 1, 2014, Sub Pop opened a new retail outlet at Seattle-Tacoma International Airport. The Sub Pop Airport Store carried Sub Pop recordings, merchandise, clothing, and books. There was also a listening station, and occasional live performances were offered as well. According to the "News" section on Sub Pop's website, Shabazz Palaces' *Lese Majesty* ranked among the "Top 3 Instant Play-n-Sell" albums, while among the "Top 3 Albums to Clear out the Store" was Earth's *Earth 2*.

The big sellers of recent years—the Shins, the Head and the Heart, Fleet Foxes—had all left Sub Pop by this point. "It's always hard when a band leaves Sub Pop," Megan admits, "but when a band that was a baby band, totally unknown to the world, becomes big on Sub Pop and then leaves the label? That can be a little harder. Although it's not easy, what we've learned over thirty years is that we all continue to evolve, and the space creates more room for other, smaller bands that might one day also become significant."

"I don't think it's a concern, really," is Tony Kiewel's view on departing bands. "We love the people we work with and always want the best for them. While I almost always think it would be best for them to stay with us, I also completely understand that the grass can often times seem greener at a major, and I don't begrudge anyone going to explore that for themselves. I am, however, also certainly not above pointing out that most of the artists who have made the jump have not, in fact, done as well as they did with us."

And, as Megan points out, some of the bands that left Sub Pop ended up returning, most notably Mudhoney. After reforming for SP20, the Afghan Whigs went on to record two more albums for Sub Pop. Sam Beam, who recorded under the name Iron & Wine (initially solo records), released three well-received albums on Sub Pop before moving to Warner Bros. Then, in 2015, Iron & Wine returned to Sub Pop with the release of *Love Letter for Fire*, followed by *Beast Epic* in 2017.

After years of inactivity, Sleater-Kinney also returned to Sub Pop in 2014, delighting their fans. The acclaimed indie rock act had switched to Sub Pop from the Kill Rock Stars record label (then based in Olympia) in 2005 for the release of their seventh album, *The Woods*. But then, while on tour the following year, the band announced they were going "on hiatus."

"I think creatively we weren't exactly sure what we would do after *The Woods*, and it felt like it was better to stop while we were ahead than to come to a grinding halt," Carrie Brownstein, one of the group's guitarists, explains. "And I think we were also just weary from the cycle of writing an album, recording an album, touring—that can become daunting. We were just ready to stop."

In 2014, the three band members decided to record again but made no public announcement about it. Instead, a one-sided single featuring the new song "Bury Our Friends" was slipped into the vinyl edition of *Start Together*, a boxed set of all the band's albums, released by Sub Pop in October 2014. Once fans realized that the song was new, the story broke: Sleater-Kinney was back. A new album, *No Cities to Love*, was released in January 2015.

◎ ◎ ◎

The *Start Together* box was only available in a limited-edition vinyl set or as a digital download, though the albums were also individually available on CD. Sub Pop had continued to release records on vinyl, even as sales dropped following the arrival of first CDs, then digital downloads. So the label was well positioned to take advantage of the resurging interest in vinyl that began happening during the first decade of the new century. In fact, it wasn't until December 2016 that Sub Pop's digital sales even surpassed the sales of physical product.

"We were doing vinyl for just about every record," Megan explains. "We still are. And the sales were going crazy, and we were having huge orders from some record stores who wanted to do exclusive runs of a certain color of vinyl record—just like the good old days. And we were selling into some accounts, like Urban Outfitters, who buy a lot of vinyl records. So we were selling more vinyl than most other labels, again, for the first time in a long time. So that's one reason why our digital numbers were as low as they were, is that our vinyl numbers were actually very high."

Sub Pop has even continued releasing cassettes. "We do almost every new release on cassette again," says Megan. "And we sell through them! Which is even weirder. We do small runs: five hundred, maybe a thousand. But they sell through."

Tony jokes that a CD resurgence is next. "If you're a punk band, and you want to get a 7-inch record to sell at your shows because you want a physical thing, it might take you six months to get those 7-inches back because the plants are so backed up," he says. "I could burn one hundred CDs in an hour, and hand draw some covers, and that to me is fucking awesome. And I can sell them for a dollar and still make a profit. And, on top of that, even old records that you used to be able to pick up at Value Village [a thrift store] for a buck apiece, now they're twenty bucks. But you could go to the CD bin section that everybody's ignoring and walk out of there with ten awesome CDs for ten bucks. Kids are going to figure that out. And they're going to figure out that a bunch of that stuff isn't on Spotify, and it is out of print, and there's actually maybe as much out-of-print stuff in those CD bins as there ever was in the LP bins. Anyway, that's my in-a-nutshell reason why CDs are awesome. CDs are punk as fuck."

Licensing and publishing have become increasingly important revenue streams for the company. "Publishing has become a bigger and bigger deal and a bigger part of the music business because while everything else is shrinking, that's growing," Tony explains. Along with income from record sales and radio airplay, "the third big chunk of money is when somebody puts a song in a TV show or a movie and they pay a fee to use that. That's the big licensing money: the car commercial. And it's less money than it used to be, but it still feels like manna from heaven."

He points to Pigeonhed's "Battle Flag" as an example. The song first appeared on the group's 1997 album *The Full Sentence*. The Lo Fidelity Allstars' remix of the track became a chart hit in both the US and UK, and was then featured in major TV shows like *ER*, *The Sopranos*, and *Smallville*, as well as numerous films and film trailers. "'Battle Flag' was such a big song for so many movie trailers," says Tony. "It made tons of money. That song probably kept the doors open for a year, I'm guessing. It was a big deal."

Sub Pop has a separate webpage for licensing (www.subpoplicensing.com) with a section listing the various placements songs have received: Band of Horses' "General Specific" in the TV show *Chuck*, Gold Leaves' "Hanging Window" in the trailer for *Brahmin Bulls*, Kelley Stoltz's "Can Do" in a commercial for BECU (Boeing Employees Credit Union). But it all comes back to having music to license in the first place.

"There's about five of us who are pretty actively pitching bands," says Tony. "We just want to work with artists that we like and respect. There's no clear directive, there's no genre. It's just, we want to back up musicians and artists who we think are cool, who want to work with us and who we share values with. And have fun doing it. There's other things that get into it; like for me, I like to challenge myself. So if I start getting bored or I feel like this is becoming too cookie cutter, I might intentionally try to do something different, like *Bob's Burgers* [Sub Pop released *The Bob's Burgers Music Album* in 2017] or something. Because it's just automatically different; you're not just putting a band on tour. How do you work singles, when clearly they're not going to be on the radio? What do you do? And so just forcing yourself into that situation keeps me excited and interested."

When he talks about bringing bands to Sub Pop, Tony makes it sound like joining a family, a team, as opposed to a purely commercial arrangement, making the case that Sub Pop is a company with an underlying sense of community. An NPR story on the label made the observation, "New acts are chosen by committee. Per the politics of the office, ownership is out. Nobody is allowed to refer to an act as 'my artist.'"

In response, Tony smiles and says, "I wouldn't say that they're 'not allowed' to, but it's frowned upon. It's just making sure that everyone here feels invested in that artist and in that relationship. This is a thing I feel like I inherited from Jonathan and Megan; it's unhealthy, I think, for a specific A&R person to feel possessive of an artist.

"Nobody is signing to Sub Pop to work with me," he continues. "They want to be on Sub Pop because it's Sub Pop, because of all the people who are here, because of the other artists who are here, because of the legacy Jonathan has built, because of the work that everyone continues to do. Yes, maybe you manage this project, or you're overseeing it, but when you start calling it 'my band,' 'my bands,' you'll see some eyebrows go up. I do think that people self-police a little bit; I don't want to slip into it, and that's the beginning of slipping into that mindset. These are all *Sub Pop* artists; these are all *our* artists.

"We really endeavor to make sure that everyone has a relationship with the artists that we work with. It's important for the artists to feel connected. It also, I think, makes them say 'yes' more often to our requests if our publicist is actually friends with this artist, and not just someone whose emails are getting forwarded by the A&R person to the manager to the artist; they might be more inclined to say 'yes,' or at least to hear why something is worth thinking about doing, when they might otherwise be like 'No, I don't want to do that—that sounds weird.' There's something that happens when you actually care about somebody that no amount of professionalism can actually create. So I really want that to be the case as much as possible. That there's emotional capital on both sides, that there's investment, personal emotional investment, going both ways. It's also more fun, like it's so much more fun when people give a shit and they're friends and it feels like family."

◉ ◉ ◉

Sub Pop started as a fanzine. As an independent record company, the label's big dreams were tempered by financial struggles, yet the label never went completely under. The sudden influx of money from the label's former acts was both a blessing and a curse; it nearly brought the label down, but again, Sub Pop managed to survive. The company also learned to navigate as the record industry moved from selling physical to digital media. Industry wide, in 2016, income from all digital platforms surpassed income from the sale of physical formats for the first time. And while major record companies have scrambled to adjust to the changing landscape, Sub Pop has managed to hold its ground and even thrive. (The label might not make much money from those runs of five hundred or one thousand cassettes, but selling them all means the company didn't lose money either.)

The alliance with Warner has also paid off, realizing the hopes of creating a label "that combines the vision of an indie and clout of a major." For Jon, that's very much the case: "Because of the unique circumstances of our partnership, Sub Pop has it both ways: it's a fully legitimate, independently owned record label that has an enduring, productive relationship with a major music company. The Warner Music Group [WMG] have been fabulous business partners: patient, helpful, and unobtrusive. In the time that WMG has been partnered with Sub Pop, WMG has had three different owners, all of whom have been cooperative. There was a time when I came to question the wisdom of having sold even the minority stake that we did—no more. The sale contributed mightily to Sub Pop's ability to become stable and flourish. Point: Sub Pop and WMG have had decades of fruitful cooperation together, and I have no reason to complain about any of it."

Sub Pop released thirty-two records in 2017, one of which, the deluxe edition of Father John Misty's *Pure Comedy*, won a Grammy for "Best Recording Package" the following year. The *Industry Observer* noted that 40 percent of the Grammy awards at the 2018 ceremony went to independent record labels, "proving that the major labels no longer have the monopolizing reach that they once did."

Being smaller than majors, independent labels can find it easier to adapt and change. Being closer to the ground, they're also better positioned to spot new talent as it emerges.

Jon contends: "The indies is where it began, and the indies is where it'll end. I think part of the reason why we've stuck around so long is because there are people around here—myself most particularly—if I wasn't doing this, I don't know what else I would do. I'm interested in all sorts of different things, but as far as a job goes, this is what I like to do.

"I quite frankly put my money where my mouth was when the company was sinking into debt; I just kinda helped keep it afloat for a number of years. But most importantly, I think it's just that the company is staffed with a bunch of passionate fans who I'm humbled to work around and who teach me things every day. Quite literally every day, I hear and learn something new, so that's like the best of all possible situations, particularly for a work environment. And I think that's why we stuck around: there's a certain amount of codependence, but a lot of passion, a lot of love, a lot of just positive expectations, and the kind of love and familial quality that, ironically, Bruce had instilled in the original mission for the company—ironically, because he's not around any more."

But it was Bruce's vision in the beginning. "That was a very surreal experience, when your dreams manifest like that," he says, looking back at the World Domination that resulted from the publication of that first thirty-two-page edition of *Subterranean Pop 1*. "Initially, with the compilations, they represented artists from around the country, and in some cases from other parts of the world. Then the label contracted into a solid regional focus. And since then it's slowly expanded to serve as a resource for a number of different artists globally."

"But it's still very much a Seattle record label," adds Jonathan.

# AFTERWORD
## Diamonds Are Forever (The Thirtieth Anniversary)

*30 years ago today: Sub Pop moved from a small apartment*
*on Capitol Hill ... to an even smaller office at 1st and Virginia.*
*Best Wishes to every fan that has ever supported an act on the*
*label, and a happy 30th anniversary to Sub Pop Records.*

—Bruce Pavitt, Facebook message, April 1, 2018

*The lease to Sub Pop's original penthouse office in the Terminal Sales*
*Building began 30 years ago today. Thus began a very long April Fools*
*prank. My love, gratitude and a hand on your wallet go out to every*
*band and band member, every fan and customer, every employee*
*and intern, every record store and distributor, every bank and creditor,*
*but mostly to our hometown of Seattle, as we begin another year (or*
*30) of celebrating, putting out records, and going out of business.*

—Jonathan Poneman, Facebook message, April 1, 2018

Sub Pop's current office is roughly midway between the plaque with Bruce and Jon's bronze footprints on Sixth Avenue and the company's original office space in the Terminal Sales Building on First Avenue. Under the name of "Sub Pop Records & Hardly Art" on the directory posted on the office building's outer door is the additional notation, "THIS LOCATION IS NOT A STORE/NOT OPEN TO THE PUBLIC," an attempt to ensure there are no more unexpected drop-in visitors.

As you walk into the office, the first thing you see is a letter board hanging on the front of the receptionist's desk welcoming visitors to Sub Pop and also noting future releases, upcoming shows, and staff birthdays. There are two gumball machines filled with white balls stamped with the Sub Pop logo. Look left as you face the desk, and on the wall you'll see neatly framed Sub Pop checks made out to Megan Jasper and her sister Maura (who'd hoped to pick up some extra money by putting in a few hours stuffing 7-inch singles into their sleeves) that bounced. "So many of my paychecks bounced!" Megan says. Today, she is Sub Pop's chief executive officer.

You'll find framed memorabilia all around the office: an invoice for the pressing of one thousand copies of *Bleach* on white vinyl ($1,100); a "LOSER" logo with a Post-it note attached instructing, "Jeff, make it BIG"; a "wooden record" award given to the Shins for *Oh, Inverted World*, when it was thought that the "indie gold" of one hundred thousand copies might be the most the album would sell, along with the official Recording Industry Association of America gold award they received when the album finally sold half a million copies. The most unusual item is probably a section of the wall from the Terminal Sales Building office with Kurt Cobain's signature and phone number; instead of simply writing the information on a piece of paper, he'd scrawled "Kurdt Kobain" on the paint-splattered wall, using one of his many varied spellings of his name. (He used this particular spelling on all of Nirvana's Sub Pop releases.)

The soda machine that used to dispense Rainier Beer is gone. But at the end of every week you'll find the staff gathering in the break room for "Wine Fridays," sharing vino and conversation. If you look out the window, you can even see the back of the Terminal Sales Building, three blocks away.

There aren't historical plaques on any of the Sub Pop offices. Nor is there one on Reciprocal Recording, which closed in 1991. It was soon reopened under the name Word of Mouth; after that, producers John Goodmanson and Stu Hallerman took it over and it became John and Stu's Place. Next up, Chris Walla, guitarist with Death Cab for Cutie, renamed it Hall of Justice Recording. Fleet Foxes took over the lease in 2008 and renamed the studio Reciprocal. Then Walla stepped in again, renovated the space, and reopened it in 2011, again as Hall of Justice Recording. If any location in Seattle deserves a historical marker, it's surely here, at the studio where recordings were made by the likes of Green River, Soundgarden, Nirvana, Mudhoney, Sleater-Kinney, Harvey Danger, Death Cab for Cutie, and Fleet Foxes—among others.

Tony Kiewel, who is now Sub Pop's co-president, says there are about forty people who work in the label's Seattle office, as well as staff at the company's warehouse in Georgetown and the employees at the Sub Pop Airport Shop. The company's director of commercial radio promotion is based in Chattanooga, Tennessee; Sub Pop Publishing is located in Los Angeles; and there's also an office in London that oversees international sales and marketing. Jon likes to point out that the staff working in Chattanooga and Los Angeles have all previously spent time working at Sub Pop's main office in Seattle.

It's another anniversary year in 2018—Sub Pop's thirtieth. On March 12, KEXP began broadcasting every Sub Pop audio release in the catalog, starting with the *Sub Pop 5* cassette. The plan is for the series to wrap up in August, when SPF30 (the "F" standing for "festival") will be held. SPF30 will include shows at the Seattle Center, the Crocodile club in downtown Seattle, a comedy show at the Moore Theatre, and a free all-day festival at Alki Beach in West Seattle. Considering that a substantial proportion of Sub Pop's staff lives in the same neighborhood, you could say that the label is throwing a party in its own backyard.

"Seattle's Alki Beach boasts some of the most awesome territorial (city/water/mountain) views the city has to offer, along with the occasional whale sighting, a somewhat diminutive replica of the Statue of Liberty, and some of the best local businesses to boot," read Sub Pop's press release about the event. "We are stoked (and not a little surprised) that the city cleared the permits."

To help smooth the way for Sub Pop's invasion of a popular public beach at the height of summer, Sub Pop's staffers have taken care to meet with neighborhood community councils, happy to share their plans and answer questions. "A question about the landscaping near the Alki Bathhouse came up, and Sub Pop said they would look at methods of protecting it from people damaging it during the event," the Westside Seattle blog wrote about such a meeting with Alki Community Council. "[Megan] Jasper said this event would require an ongoing conversation and vowed to come back to the group and update them on progress as more details were confirmed. The number of shuttles, how water traffic might be handled, and other core issues are still being nailed down."

"Georgetown felt magical to me. Marymoor Park was pretty amazing, too," says Tony about Sub Pop's previous festivals, while looking forward to SPF30. "And I'll tell you, as much as I think it's an exciting thing, a gift to give to the community that has been so gracious to Sub Pop over the years, I think everyone here will tell you their favorite thing is seeing all the bands in one place. Because that's the thing that doesn't happen as often. It's all these people that we love, that we have grown super close to, that we maybe have met once or twice, and getting to have a full day of hanging out and watching each other play and getting drunk. Especially now that there's no CMJ [*College Music Journal*] showcases and South by Southwest [the annual music and film festival in Austin, Texas] is always such a scramble. So there's just fewer of those opportunities left. It's a big deal for us."

Sub Pop Records is in good, stable shape as it heads into the future, ably guided by the core trio of Jon (though still Executive Chairman of Supervisory Management at heart, his official titles are co-president and chairman), Megan, and Tony. Megan, in her second term at the label, has now been by Jon's side for over two decades—longer than he managed with Bruce.

Megan, who's risen from senior product manager, to general manager, to executive vice-president, to CEO, says, "I have to tell you, I don't feel like my job changed a ton with the title changes. My job for so many years was to understand Jonathan's vision and to execute it. And I still feel like that will always be my job. For the most part, I help to create and set an agenda. I identify our priorities as a label, and a company. I check back in with different teams to make sure that everything is operating the way things need to operate in order to move forward. I spend a lot of my time troubleshooting or problem solving with individuals or groups or departments. I try to make sure that we are set up in a way that feels responsible, financially. I scrutinize what we're spending. It's like running a household, except it's just a business."

Asked about Sub Pop's current vision, she says, "When we talk about it now, we talk about things in terms of 'core business.' That's the part of the vision that will never change; it's like a mission statement. And the core business is the signing of artists that we can develop. So I would say that that part of our vision is still intact and still remains; signing great artists that we can amplify out into the world.

"And then I would also say that what's new as far as our vision goes is understanding, guiding, and respecting the brand. We didn't have to think like that fifteen or twenty years ago. Well, we did, but we did it differently. Before, we knew that our brand was only a reflection of the bands that we worked with. And that's not totally the case anymore, and that's not for any reason other than aging. When something is thirty years old, what Sub Pop is to one person is different to what it is to another person. And we have to be mindful of that. And we have to guide things in a way that feels respectful of what the brand is."

As Megan astutely recognizes, today, "Sub Pop" is a brand that exists quite distinct from its artists. It's the realization of Bruce's original dream for Sub Pop: that the label would have a resonance akin to Motown or Blue Note, where the name itself signified a particular aesthetic as much as—or even more than—the artists on that label. But what does it mean to run a record company at a time when record companies are seen by some as irrelevant?

"There are times where we get a little bit nervous," Tony admits. "Like, what's going on in the business? What's going on in the industry? Is whatever our particular niche we fill in the music industry going to be filled in by this whole other kind of business? I think there's always been a set of challenges. But what keeps us feeling relatively secure is that we're willing to bet [on an act] earlier than most other labels, so that's one advantage that we have.

"Second is, the services that we offer under the umbrella of being a record label are still things that bands want to have happen for them. Yeah, you can still put your stuff on Bandcamp, and somebody may care about it. But maybe not. Most bands still want to have a publicist; most bands still want their music sent to college radio—at least the bands we work with. Most bands still want somebody pitching their songs to Subaru commercials or *This Is Us* episodes, or whatever it is. Most people want to have CDs and LPs made. And that all by itself is a considerable amount of work and upfront investment. So, as long as bands still need those things done and need help doing them, then that's where we fit in. When they stop wanting that stuff, then we might be in trouble.

"But I feel like that's why we have tried to maintain our identity as a company, why we do care about our logo and what Sub Pop means, and what our merchandise looks like that uses our logo, and why we are constantly expanding and evolving our merchandise. So there's these sort of safety nets that we've set up for ourselves that are not just safety nets, they're becoming core businesses. But at the end of the day, our absolute core business is finding artists and championing them to the best of our ability, because that's also why most of us get up in the morning and what makes us interested in this job. This is how we figured out how to be a part of it."

Jon, too, feels there are practical reasons why there's a need for record companies in general, and Sub Pop in particular, to exist. "Our job is much broader than it used to be," he says. "Selling music in the second decade of the twenty-first century is very different than when Bruce and I started doing it in 1988. It used to be that it was very monolithic; you would have retail, and you had six major labels, and a handful of indies who were able to get their records into this closed retail environment, and that's how people got music out. And now, obviously, with the online opportunities for self-marketing, to say nothing of the digital music providers, there's so many different ways that one can approach the music industry. But I think there's a need for record companies from the standpoint that for the artists that we work with, they find a tremendous amount of value in working with us because we have expertise, relationships, and in some cases money, which is in many cases what a lot of the artists need to get going."

Something else that has helped keep Sub Pop fresh and dynamic is the company's interest in continually moving forward, developing new artists and new relationships. Jon speaks with pride about having helped KEXP establish ties with the Polish music industry, as a result of his own visits to the country. (His wife, Magdalena, is a Polish national.) "And it's just one small country out of a planet full of so many rich and diverse cultures. But to be able to get KEXP over there; it's not important for music as a phenomenon, or even for this label's survival. But it's little things like that—little accomplishments—that for me are very profound. Because the more avenues that we can open up into the unexpected, the more interesting and vital I think our job, and the things that we're trying to accomplish, become.

"It's very rewarding to have the Afghan Whigs come back and make great records on Sub Pop, and the same thing with Sam [Beam]. But the more interesting thing to me are bands like King Tuff, or the Dum Dum Girls—or a band that's kind of right in the middle of both those worlds. Sleater-Kinney, who wasn't originally on Sub Pop, they started on the label with *The Woods*, and they've been doing great things. That's been very exciting—a privilege to be part of."

"The rise of the Internet has changed more than simply the way music is sold and distributed. It's also profoundly changed the ways in which we communicate with each other. Bruce's original inspiration was the championing of regional music scenes, at a time when a person's exposure to such music was limited, especially if you didn't live close to a record shop that carried independently released music, or within broadcast range of a radio station like KAOS. But post-Internet, can it be said that any region of the country, or the world, is truly that isolated?

"With the rise of the web, organic regional scenes can no longer occur," contends Daniel House. "Because the band now has a global platform to do whatever they're doing. All the biggest regional scenes have happened in isolation. I actually think that the Seattle grunge scene is probably going to be the last real occurrence like that, of its kind. I think there'll still be big bands, but I don't think there'll be big regional scenes, in that way. And as a result, I don't think there will be regional independent labels that sort of reflect a scene.

"Think back then: all the indie labels, whether they were regional or bigger than that, they were either regionally specific, or they had a specific kind of aesthetic. And now if you have a Melvins or a Malfunkshum or a Skin Yard or a Green River or a U-Men in some scene, they're no longer relegated to obscurity, because they have Bandcamp, they have SoundCloud, they have all these different venues that they can put their music on and get picked up. If they're doing something innovative, they can put it up on SoundCloud, and all of a sudden in Poland or in Italy or Canada—there's all these fans picking up on what they're doing."

Of course, as Tony points out, just because you have a song on Bandcamp doesn't mean that anyone's going to find it and listen to it; that's where a record label can step in and help with promotion. But it's certainly true that a music scene can no longer develop in isolation; a band's first efforts in the studio or onstage can be shared via social media instantaneously.

Sub Pop's story is not just the story of a record label and the high-profile acts the label discovered. It's also the story of the kind of record label that wouldn't be launched for the same reasons anymore. Sub Pop was very much a product of its time, when music scenes felt like small communities. Today, Seattle itself has been transformed into a bustling metropolis, home to Amazon and numerous Internet and technology companies (and, unfortunately, also struggling with the problems endemic to large cities, among them, income inequality, traffic gridlock, and homelessness). Yet Sub Pop still feels like a small community. "It's kind of a cliché for companies like ours, but there's a real familial aspect to it," Jon agrees.

"Like a human being, the label has had stages of development," Jon said about Sub Pop in 2013. "We had a rocky adolescence, and now we're kind of going through a flirtation with maturity." In the same interview, he looked, typically, to the future. "We're always trying to stay inspired in a genuine way, and that will inevitably mean a shifting of perspective for the label. We're proud of our history and the legacy that we share with the city of Seattle, but we're always looking forward. That, to me, is always the exciting thing."

And, in a positive development from the early days, fiscal accountability now plays an important role in how the company operates. "It's important to us to be doing good business," says Jon, "and to run the place with an attention paid to the bottom line, and trying to do things, fulfill our mission, in the most responsible way possible." Such an attitude of responsibility also bodes well for Sub Pop's future.

Thirty-eight years after Bruce's *Subterranean Pop #1* appeared in May 1980, Sub Pop is an established record label that continues to flourish. And Jon has every intention of seeing that it remains so. "To me, the most important thing you can do is just put your head down, and endure, and carry on, and do your job, and enjoy your job, and love your city. And that's what I do."

And though Bruce is no longer directly involved with the company's affairs, he remains very interested in seeing what his creation has become. Knowing the difficulties involved in not only becoming successful, but also remaining successful, he has an understandable pride and admiration for what Sub Pop has been able to accomplish, both with and without him.

"I'll tell you, running a record label, trying to keep a record label alive, is very, very challenging," he says. "It's an industry based on whim and fashion and you never know when the next hit record's going to come or the next major act is going to tank. So it's a real rollercoaster. I would say that Sub Pop has found a real happy medium. And they've continued to put out a lot of good records."

# ACKNOWLEDGMENTS

First, profound thanks to Nick Soulsby for getting the ball rolling by recommending me to Scott B. Bomar and Kate Hyman at BMG. Further thanks to Scott for closing the deal and giving me the opportunity to write this book, and being so understanding throughout the process. Thanks to Tom Seabrook for his editing. My work was greatly enhanced by the cooperation of Sub Pop's co-founders, Bruce Pavitt and Jonathan Poneman; many thanks to both of you, your help was much appreciated! Thanks also to those who agreed to new interviews: Nils Bernstein, Jack Endino, Daniel House, Megan Jasper, Rich Jensen, Tony Kiewel, Steve Manning, Charles Peterson, and Dan Trager. I also drew on my archival interviews with Bruce and Jon, as well as Mark Arm, Carrie Brownstein, Kurt Danielson, Jack Endino, Charles Peterson, and Kim Thayil. Thanks to Fred Mills for assigning me to write a series of stories about the SP20 festival back in 2008; who knew they would prove to be so useful ten years on? Thanks to Mike Ziegler, for his help with the music. And thanks to Jacob McMurray at the Museum of Pop Culture for allowing me access to the museum's oral history archives.

# BIBLIOGRAPHY

**Books**

Azerrad, Michael. *Come As You Are: The Story of Nirvana*. New York: Main Street Books, 1994.

Cameron, Keith. *Mudhoney: The Sound and the Fury from Seattle*. Minneapolis: Voyageur Press, 2014.

Gaar, Gillian G. *Entertain Us: The Rise of Nirvana*. London: Jawbone Press, 2012.

Neely, Kim. *Five Against One: The Pearl Jam Story*. New York: Penguin Books, 1998.

Nickson, Chris. *Soundgarden: New Metal Crown*. New York: St. Martin's Press, 1995.

Pavitt, Bruce. *Experiencing Nirvana: Grunge in Europe, 1989*. Brooklyn: Bazillion Points, 2013.

Pavitt, Bruce. *Sub Pop USA: The Subterranean Pop Music Anthology, 1980–1988*. Brooklyn: Bazillion Points, 2014.

Peterson, Charles. *Screaming Life: A Chronicle of the Seattle Music Scene*. San Francisco: HarperCollinsWest, 1995.

Peterson, Charles. *Touch Me I'm Sick*. New York: powerHouse Books, 2003.

Prato, Greg. *Grunge Is Dead: The Oral History of Seattle Rock Music*. Toronto, Canada: ECW Press, 2009.

Whitburn, Joel. *Top Pop Albums*. Menomonee Falls, Wisconsin: Record Research Inc., 2010.

Whitburn, Joel. *Top Pop Singles 1955–2015*. Menomonee Falls, Wisconsin: Record Research Inc., 2016.

White, Emily. *You Will Make Money in Your Sleep: The Story of Dana Giacchetto, Financial Adviser to the Stars*. New York: Scribner, 2007.

Yarm, Mark. *Everybody Loves Our Town: An Oral History of Grunge*. New York: Crown Archetype, 2011.

## Articles

Alden, Grant. "Sub Plop?," *The Rocket*, August 1991.

Appelo, Tim. "Sub Pop Looks Back, Celebrates 25 Years With 40,000-Strong Silver Jubilee Celebration," *Billboard*, July 16, 2013.

Appelo, Tim, and Gary Baum. "From Mike Ovitz to Leonardo DiCaprio: A Wall Street Criminal Recalls His Hollywood Heyday," *Hollywood Reporter*, April 18, 2014.

Azerrad, Michael. "Grunge City," *Rolling Stone*, April 16, 1992.

Beckmann, Jim. "KEXP & Sub Pop Present Mudhoney on the Space Needle!," blog. kexp.org, July 10, 2013.

Bienstock, Richard. "Excerpt: Kim Thayil on the Secrets Behind His Tunings," guitarworld.com, November 12, 2012.

Boss, Kit. "Young, Loud, and Snotty," *Seattle Times*, August 24, 1989.

Boyer, Richy. "Hell's Angels," *The Rocket*, October 7, 1998.

Brickner, Sara. "Sub Pop's Hardly Art Is Hardly Starving," *Seattle Weekly*, September 15, 2009.

Brodeur, Nicole. "Sub Pop Founder Finds Calm in Dire Diagnosis," *Seattle Times*, May 31, 2013.

Brodeur, Nicole. "The Queen of Capitol Hill," *Seattle Times*, June 10, 2013.

Brodeur, Nicole. "Sub Pop Founders Find a Step on Nordstrom Walk of Fame," *Seattle Times*, April 14, 2014.

Cameron, Keith. "Spirit of '88," *Mojo*, August 2008.

Chrisfield, Bryget and Uppy Chatterjee. "The Shins Frontman Admits He Regrets That Maccas Commercial After All," theMusic.com, May 3, 2017.

Crock, Jason. "Bruce Pavitt and Jon Poneman," *Pitchfork*, July 7, 2008.

Cross, Charles R. "Sub Pop Cans Four," *The Rocket*, March 12, 1997.

De Barros, Paul. "Meet the Punk Who Saved Sub Pop," *Seattle Times*, June 9, 2013.

De Revere, Paul. "Sub Pop Throw Themselves a Silver Jubilee," rollingstone.com, July 11, 2013.

Douglas, Martin. "An Incredible Exercise in Diplomacy: Talking Label Management with Sarah Moody of Hardly Art Records," forbes.com, March 29, 2016.

Douglas, Martin. "Ishmael Butler Comes Down to Earth," *Seattle Weekly*, July 12, 2017.

Dunn, Collin. "Recording a Renewable Record: Kelley Stoltz," treehugger.com, March 10, 2006.

Edwards, Gavin. "Fortune Flows from Grungy Beginnings," *Los Angeles Times*, January 8, 2012.

Ehrbar, Joe. "Sub Pop: New Dawning Time," *The Rocket*, April 7, 1999.

Elliott, Gwendolyn. "Sub Pop Imprint Hardly Art Celebrates 10 Years as a Tastemaker All Its Own," daily.bandcamp.com, May 1, 2017.

Ellis-Petersen, Hannah. "Streaming Growth Helps Digital Music Revenues Surpass Physical Sales," *Guardian*, April 12, 2016.

Emery, Patrick. "From Pissing Off PA Stacks to Possible Death Hoaxes: Blag Dahlia Takes Us Through the History of Dwarves," beat.com/au.

Endelman, Michael. "Postal Service Drops Lawsuit Against Band Namesake," *Entertainment Weekly*, November 12, 2004.

Erdman, Derek. "Slavin' for Losers: What It's like to Work as the Receptionist at Sub Pop Records," *The Stranger*, July 10, 2013.

Fennessy, Kathy. "King Tuff and More at the Jubilee," thestranger.com/lineout, July 14, 2013.

Franzman, Erin. "Your Favorite Label Sucks," *The Stranger*, November 11, 1999.

Gaar, Gillian. "Sub Pop, Nirvana, and 90s Guitar Rock," *Record Collector*, November 1992.

Gaar, Gillian G. "C/Z," *Goldmine*, March 18, 1994.

Gaar, Gillian G. "Independence Is Best," *Goldmine*, May 13, 2005.

Gaar, Gillian G. "Exclusive Report: Sub Pop 20, Thurs./Fri.," blurtonline.com, July 12, 2008.

Gaar, Gillian G. "Exclusive Report: Sub Pop 20, Sun.," blurtonline.com, July 24, 2008.

Gaar, Gillian G. "Sub Pop Grunge Parade Pt. 1: Green River," blurtonline.com, August 18, 2008

Gray, Tyler. "Punk Rock Branding: How Bruce Pavitt Built Sub Pop in an Anti-Corporate Nirvana," fastcompany.com, November 29, 2012.

Hann, Michael. "Sub Pop: 25 Years of Underground Rock," *Guardian*, July 4, 2013.

Heater, Brian. "Sailing the Sea of Pennies: Sub Pop's Digital Salvation," engadget.com, July 25, 2013.

Hendrickson, Matt. "Sub Popped?," *Rolling Stone*, November 12, 1998.

Hirshberg, Glen. "Is Sub Pop About to Pop?," *Seattle Weekly*, October 23, 1991.

Howell, Steve. "From Toledo Ground to the Seattle Sound," musicnotesandquotes.com.

Jenke, Tyler. "This Year's Grammy Awards Was Huge for Independent Labels," *Industry Observer*, February 1, 2018.

Jewell, Sean. "Drunk On Sub Pop Silver Jubilee's Pop Stage," thestranger.com/lineout, July 7, 2013.

Kaufman, Gil. "The Sub Pop Records 'Mutiny,'" mtv.com, March 5, 1997.

Kugiya, Hugo. "Beyond Grunge at Sub Pop: Back to Work, The Party's Over," *Pacific Magazine*, August 11, 1996.

Landler, Mark. "The Media Business: The Music, and the Dissonance, at Time Warner," *New York Times*, November 17, 1995.

Lichtman, Irv. "The Billboard Bulletin: Warner Stake in Sub Pop," *Billboard*, December 3, 1994.

Marin, Rick. "Grunge: Success for the Great Unwashed," *New York Times*, November 15, 1992.

Martens, Todd. "Q&A: Jonathan Poneman," *Billboard*, August 20, 2005.

Masters, Marc. "What's This Generation Coming To?: The Sub Pop Singles Club," *Pitchfork*, July 8, 2008.

Masuo, Sandy. "The Sub Pop System," *Musician*, December 1992.

Matson, Andrew. "Seattle Shakeup: How Sub Pop Changed Again in 2011," *The Record*, npr.com, December 29, 2011.

McNair, James. "On the hunt for meaning with Seattle band Fleet Foxes," *Independent*, June 13, 2008.

Moe, Pete. "Bruce & Jon: Game Over," *Hype*, December 1992.

Morris, Chris. "Sub Pop Stays True to Roots as It Branches Beyond Seattle," *Billboard*, July 17, 1993.

Morris, Chris. "Sub Pop to Be Distributed By ADA," *Billboard*, October 23, 1993.

Nelson, Sean. "Hardly Art Records," *The Stranger*, September 14, 2016.

Nokes, Emily. "20 Years of Linda's Tavern," *The Stranger*, February 12, 2014.

Pattison, Louis. "Did You Hear the One About Sub Pop Doing Comedy?," *Guardian*, September 14, 2014.

Paynter, Susan. "Musician's Death Hoax Not So Funny," *Seattle Post-Intelligencer*, September 1, 1993.

Peisner, David. "Fleet Foxes and the Year's Most Beautiful Album," *Spin*, May, 2011.

Poneman, Jonathan. "Grunge & Glory," *Vogue*, December 1992.

Romano, Mike. "Sub Pop Had a Great Fall," *Seattle Weekly*, March 26, 1997.

Romano, Tricia. "Shabazz Palaces Shake Up Seattle's Hip-Hop Scene," npr.org, August 1, 2014.

Rose, Cynthia. "Legend of Fallout Records, Books & Comics Evolves as Energetic New Owner Takes Over Capitol Hill Store," *Seattle Times*, August 27, 1999.

Segal, Dave. "Touch Me, I'm Sub Pop's Warehouse Manager," *The Stranger*, August 29, 2012.

Segal, Dave. "KEXP to Play Tracks Off Every Release on Sub Pop to Celebrate the Label's 30th Anniversary," thestranger.com, March 20, 2018.

Sisario, Ben. "Postal Service Tale: Indie Rock, Snail Mail, and Trademark Law," *New York Times*, November 6, 2004.

Sommerfeld, Seth. "A Fiendish Conversation with Sub Pop's Jonathan Poneman," seattlemet.com, July 8, 2013.

Sternthots, Salty. "Another Room," punks-on-acid/blogspot.com, September 2, 2016.

Stosuy, Brandon. "Jonathan Poneman," *Pitchfork*, July 29, 2013.

True, Everett. "Mudhoney: Sub Pop, Sub Normal, Subversion!," *Melody Maker*, March 11, 1989.

True, Everett. "Sub Pop: Seattle: Rock City," *Melody Maker*, March 18, 1989.

Ugwu, Reggie. "Sub Pop Signs Shabazz Palaces' Ishmael Butler to A&R Team," *New York Times*, August 12, 2013.

Vaughn, Rob. "Discography: Sub Pop Discography, Part One," groups.google.com/forum/#!topic/rec.music.info/CRgQSQ8VJ1Q

Wilson, Geordie. "Local Record Label Sues Distributor," *Seattle Times*, July 17, 1993.

Wilson, Kathleen. "Three Less at Sub Pop," *The Stranger*, November 20, 1997.

Wilson, Kathleen. "Die Young Stay Angry," *The Stranger*, April 24, 2003.

Zwickel, Jonathan. "The Seattle Band the Head and the Heart Prepares Itself for Something Big," *Seattle Times*, October 16, 2010.

——— "Independent Labels Account for Over 40% of Wins at 60th Annual GRAMMY Awards," a2im.org, January 29, 2018.

——— "Listeners Won't 'Give Up' on Postal Service," billboard.com, August 5, 2004.

——— "Sub Pop's Alki Party," westseattleblog.com, March 13 2018.

——— "Sub Pop Co-Founder Looks Forward to Next 25 Years," *Canadian Press*, cbc.ca, August 12, 2013.

——— "Sub Pop Records Sets New Industry Standard By 'Greening' Label with the Bonneville Environmental Foundation," resource-solutions.org, July 31, 2006.

——— "UO Interviews: Sub Pop Records," blog.urbanoutfitters.com.

## Websites

billboard.com

cycletheory.tripod.com/discography/singlesclub.html

hardlyart.com

mudhoneysite.com

ocf.berkeley.edu/~ptn/mudhoney/

pettediscographies.com/subpop.asp

popsike.com/Sub-Pop-Singles-Club-over-125-45s-nearly-complete-set/4064898137.html

web.stargate.net

subpop.com

subpoplicensing.com

youtube.com

wikipedia.com

# INDEX